NAXOS
& MINOR CYCLADES

EDITIONS
TOUBI'S
ΕΚΔΟΣΕΙΣ

© Copyright   MICHAEL TOUBIS PUBLICATIONS S.A.
                 Nisiza Karela, Koropi, Attiki.
                 Telephone: +30 210 6029974, Fax: +30 210 6646856
                 Web Site: http://www.toubis.gr

ISBN: 960-540-376-5

...Morning colours dissolved in the water's
Conflagrations of sunsets on the backs of seagulls,
Masts pointing to the infinite
Open thresholds to the steps of night
And over the sleep of stone
In mid-air, in full light, incessant
The song of the sea
Entering through the small windows
Designing gardens, reflections and dreams
On the silent window panes on the slumbering foreheads...

Yiannis Ritsos
(From 'March of the Ocean')

*N*axos has always been known to archaeologists, historians, students of folklore and all those who, wherever they may find themselves, are capable of discovering places of beauty and magic.

Yet to the thousands of tourists from Greece and abroad who flock to the island in the summer, Naxos has always been and remains pretty much undiscovered. This applies even to quite a number of the islanders themselves, who, tied down by the routine of daily life in the provinces, do not have the time to explore the byways of their homeland so as to appreciate it better.

This author was fortunate enough to be able to watch from close quarters some of the archaeological excavations carried out on Naxos in the past, to hold some of the stone inscriptions in his hands, to be present when the pottery was being restored and reassembled in the Museum, to meet some of the archaeologists -almost mythical figures at the time- and to participate in hours and hours of conversation and debate about Naxos.

The Professor of Archaeology from Athens University photographed the kouros - as statues of young men were called in antiquity - at Melanes. He made a student stand next to it, however, so that the photograph would give an idea of its giant size and convey a sense of the monumental nature of this work of sculpture. Elsewhere, a whole team of workmen are labouring in the Kastro's, the Castle's, one remaining tower. You climb the tower to gaze out over the ocean, sit in the enormous hall, climb up and down the stairs and explore the attics, the secret apartments and the dungeons. You encounter the coats of arms of the families who lived here and feel as if the clock had turned back and you are in the world of the Venetian nobles.

It was experiences such as those which made the author to want to show Naxos to his friends as he himself experienced and felt it. Above all, it was the author's wish to convey to a wider public the findings of the experts who have in the past investigated Naxos and its history.

The idea of writing this book was a challenge. Certain things that had been discussed and observed with groups of friends in the summer, on excursions all over the island, which had to be put down on paper and shared with others, without losing the tone of familiarity which is best suited to friends on a trip together.

As everywhere else, a guidebook is not the end of one's acquaintance with Naxos it is just a good starting-point. We would like to begin this guidebook, first and foremost, with an expression of its author's affection for and appreciation of Naxos and its inhabitants.

Sophia A. Katsourou
Constantinos A. Katsouros

CONTENTS

NAXOS

1. INTRODUCTION

2. HISTORY

3. CULTURE AND TRADITION

4. A TOUR OF NAXOS

CONTENTS

Hora.

1 NAXOS

«...This island possessed great sweetness and tranquillity.
Everywhere huge piles of melons, peaches and figs, surrounded by a calm sea.
I looked at the inhabitants. Their faces were kindly; they had never been frightened
by Turks or earthquakes, and their eyes were not on fire. Liberty here had extinguished the yearning
for liberty. Life extended like a sheet of contented, slumbering water,
which, though turbulent at times, never raised a true tempest.
As I walked about Naxos, security was the island's first gift that I became aware of.»

(Nikos Kazantzakis, Report to Greco, trans. P.A. Bien)

the «happy island»

Kazantzakis was right: it is a feeling of security and stability which one feels when one first sees Naxos, as a dim line on the horizon, from the boat.

You do not yet know, of course, what the island will be like, whether it will appeal to you.

You still have within you the memory of the last stop at Paros, with the gentleness of Parikia and the whiteness of Naousa. Already, however, the magnificence of Naxos which is, after all, the largest of the Cycladic islands can be sensed. There are towering mountains, and if you are lucky enough to arrive on a clear day the summit of Mt Zas tallest in the Cyclades at 1,004 metres, can be seen. Those mountains are perhaps what lends a feeling of security to the island realm of the Cyclades, which are

otherwise dominated by the gnawing sea and salt and the burning sun. At last the voyage is over and you disembark to find yourself in a bustling little town.

There really are «huge piles» of melons, peaches and figs, as well as oranges, potatoes, grapes, tomatoes, cheese and all the other good things that Providence showers on the island. The produce of Naxos can be found not only on the island itself or on its neighbours, but as far away as Athens.

The sea, too, really is calm. Not that this implies any absence of wind; we are, after all, in the middle of the Aegean, and that means gales. Whatever time of the year you visit Naxos, you are sure to feel the touch of wild northerly, southerly, and south-westerly winds. But Naxos has beaches which are safe and beautiful, despite the open sea, and you will surely find them.

Any visitor who wants to really get to know Naxos will have to be prepared to move around, to go beyond the familiar roads in the vicinity of Hora (as the main town is traditionally called in all the islands) and enter the heart of Naxos. That means passing through the Sea Gate, which leads to the old market, the Castle Gate which is the portal of Marco Sanudo's mediaeval town and, above all, leaving Hora behind you altogether to explore the rest of the island.

Nature and Location

Geographical features

Naxos is one of the Cycladic islands and is part of the Prefecture of the Cyclades. It lies a short distance to the east of Paros whilst to its south and south-west are the islands of Irakleia, Schinousa, Epano Koufonisi, Kato Koufonisi, Keros, and Ano and Kato Antikeri. To the east are the islets of Makares, Ayia Paraskevi, Strongili and Donousa.

Naxos is round in shape. It has a length from north to south of 17.6 miles and a greatest width, approximately in the centre, of 13.2 miles. It covers a total area of 430 square metres and its coastline is 148 kilometres long. If we were to sail around the island from the north coast in a south-westerly direction then we would encounter the bays of Limeneri, Kyra, Amyti, Ayios Georgios and Kyrades, the islets of Amarantes, Aspronisi and Parthenos, and the capes Kavos Mikris Viglas, Kouroupia and Katomeri (south). The east coast of Naxos is not as interestingly formed, with the exceptions of the capes of Axala and Kavo Stavro. The island is mountainous and a tall mountain range runs across the whole of the island, from the south to the north. The tallest peak is Mt Zeus (1,003 metres), which lies somewhere in the middle of the mountain range. Other peaks are Koronos (997 m.), Anathematistra (778 m.), Mavrovouni (869 m.), Troullos (606 m.), Kerasea (523 m.), Mavri Petra (420 m.), Paliopyrgos (227 m.) and Viglatouri (418 m.).

Naxos has fertile earth and produces significant quantities of cereals, olive oil, fruit and wine. Livestock farming is also quite developed, producing select quality cheeses, as are tourism and the processing of agricultural produce. The main source of income, however, is emery ('Naxiot earth'), which is mined in the north-east. A fine marble is also found in the mountain regions. According to the census of 1981, Naxos had 14,037 inhabitants.

Administration

In the past Naxos consisted of a municipality and many autonomous communities. The recent 'Capodistrias' programme for the redistribution of local administration created two large municipalities, the Municipality of Naxos, which includes Hora (the main town) and the surrounding areas, and the Municipality of Drymalia, which contains the former autonomous communities of the villages of Filoti, Apeiranthos, Koronos, Komiaki, Halki (Tragaia) and Moni. The other communities have remained as they were. The Municipality of Naxos is very developed and has recently made important advances in tourism as well, all the income from which goes directly to the municipal purse. The Municipality of Drymalia includes the most developed villages of mountain Naxos, the residents of which look to improving their quality of life, developing their crops and agriculture and other sectors

Climate

The climate of Naxos is mild and is similar to that of central Greece. The winter is cold, but not especially so. The summer is quite hot with plenty of sunshine, although the atmosphere is cooled down by the northerly summer winds, which start in the first days of August.

LEGEND

Asphalt road

Non-asphalt road

Ferry route

Church

Archaeological site

Cave

Beach

Airport

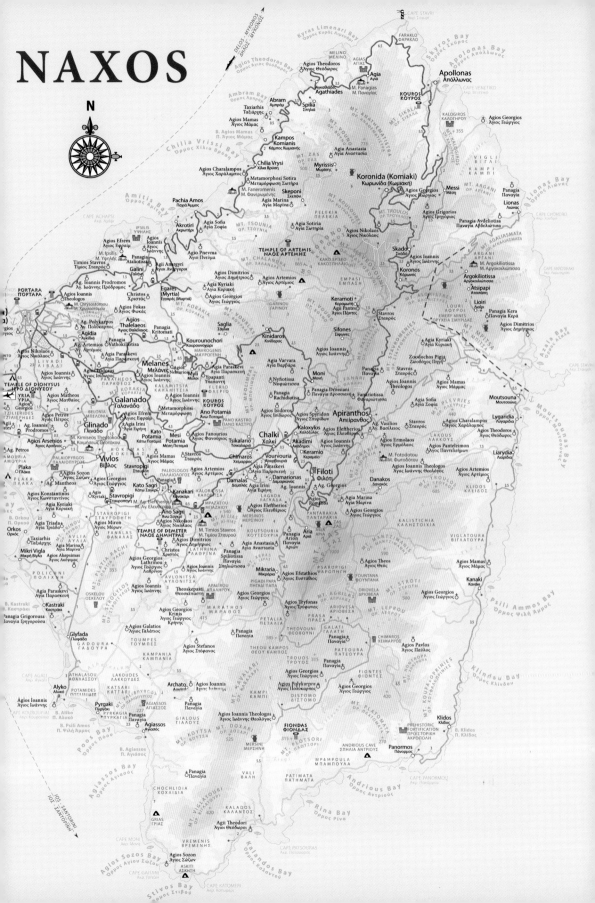

The natural environment

In much earlier geological eras, Naxos was unified with the rest of the Cycladic islands in one area of dry land, whilst even earlier before this the island's mountains were part of a continuous stretch which covered the whole of the area of today's Aegean sea. Later, the sea level rose and Naxos became an island. Today, it is the largest of the Cycladic islands. It is round in shape and its eastern section is covered by a low mountain range, including the mountains Koronos (997 m.), Mavrovouni (867 m.) and Zas (1001 m.).

In the prehistoric era, Naxos was covered with dense forest in which lived a rich fauna of mammals and birds. These forests were preserved at many points of the island until the Middle Ages, as was part of its ancient fauna too. Even in the Frankish period (13th - 16th centuries) travellers were impressed by the large animals on the island, such as jackal and deer.

Plenty of birds also resided permanently on the island or passed through whilst on their migratory journeys. Melchisedech Thevenot, who travelled through Naxos in the 17th century, was impressed by the large number of chukars (Alectoris chukar). In his day there were still deer on Naxos, even though the island had been stripped bare of its forest by then.

Today, the mountains of Naxos are completely bare of forest; the most dominant type of vegetation is dry bushes whilst in some areas bushes of holly, filikia, tsikoudia and other types of Mediterranean maquis bush still survive.

In the flat areas and the valleys there are many crops with olives and citrus fruits whilst the slopes of the hills are still cultivated with the system of built raised platforms (low walls). Vines and various vegetables are grown in this way.

The potatoes of Naxos, a local variety which is easy to cultivate, are well-known throughout Greece. Uncontrolled livestock rearing has caused much harm to the natural vegetation of the island. Even so, a large number of small plants continues to survive, such as anemones (Anemone pavonina), lupins (Lupinus graecus), sowbreads (Cyclamen hederifolium), corn poppies (Papaver rhoeas), stock (Matthiola sinuata), camomile (Anthemis chia), vetchlings, fenugreek, vetch and many others.

We should also mention some bulbous plants, such as the crocuses Colchium variegatum, Crocus laevigatus and the Crocus tournefortii, and at least 15 kinds of orchid.

Many rare species of plant grow on Mount Zas, such as the treacle mustard (Erysimum naxense) and the comfrey (Symphytum naxicola), which are endemic to Naxos, and the chickweed (Cerastium runemarkii), Bupleurum aira, Asperula abbreviata, bellflower (Campanula calaminthifolia), snowdrop (Galanthus ikariae subsp snogerupii) and others, which are endemic to the Cyclades.

In the coastal zone we encounter plants that have adjusted to the saline conditions of the sea water. These include the sea daffodil (Pancratium maritimum), the three-horned stock (Matthiola tricuspidata), the sea holly (Glaucium flavum), the rock samphire (Crithmum maritimum), the virginia stock (Malcolmia flexuousa subsp. naxensis) and many others.

As for fauna, it is well known that in the mountains of the island there are many peregrines (Falco peregrinus), Bonelli's eagles (Hieraaetus fasciatus), long-legged buzzards (Buteo rufinus) and many other birds of prey, whilst in the past there were also griffon vultures (Gyps fulvus), which now appear to have become extinct. Other rare birds are the Eleonora's falcon (Falco eleonorae) and Audouin's gull (Larus audouini), two types characteristic of the Aegean. This does not include, of course, the many migratory birds that pass through the island every spring and autumn. Unfortunately, uncontrolled hunting means that many types of bird are on the verge of extinction.

The only serious effort that has been made for the protection of the environment are the projects that took place in the mountain village of Apeiranthos on the initiative of the former mayor Manolis Glezos. Small dams retain the rain water and enrich the water-level in the soil, whilst the raised platforms were replaced and there was a return to traditional forms of cultivation, as in the old days.

The eastern mountain range of Naxos, Mts Mavrovouni and Zas and the uninhabited southern area as far as cape Katomeri are protected areas under the European Union's 'Natura 2000' programme.

Geology

Geologically, the island of Naxos is part of the Attic-Cycladic Complex. This is a former continent that was made up of the Cyclades, southern Euboia and Attica. Generally speaking, the Attic-Cycladic Complex contains metamorphic rocks. These are rocks that have been subject to high pressures and temperatures as a result of having been submerged during the formation of the mountains in the lower levels of the earth's crust. During the metamorphosis of the rocks, the minerals and rocks are re-crystallised, there is intense schist-production activity and the creation of new minerals with the exchange of material. The rocks that were formed during this process of metamorphosis can be either sedimentary deposits or new formations and date to as early as the Mesozoic period, i.e. 245 - 130 million years ago. Only one section of these, the lowest strata, is older and is estimated to be 355 million years old, formed during the Palaeozoic era.

As such, the rocks that we see in Naxos today were first metamorphosed between 40 and 45 million years ago, during the period known as the mid-Eocene. During this first phase of metamorphosis it is calculated that the rocks were submerged 40-50 thousand metres below the earth's surface.

The second phase of metamorphosis took place in the region 25 million years ago, during the Oligocene period. These rocks came to the surface during the formation of the Alpine orogenic system. In addition, with the submergence of the rocks and the parallel rising of the earth's crust, an infiltration of granite magma took place concurrently.

A third phase of metamorphosis occurred 17 million years ago and was characterised by high temperatures and the infiltration of granitic diorites.

Almost the whole of the island of Naxos, then, is made up of metamorphic rock, such as: marble, granite, schist, gneisses, amphibolites and migmatites. Moreover, there has been an infiltration of magma, creating the granite which makes up one-third of the island, whilst almost the whole of the rest of Naxos is made up of crystallised schist and marble.

2   Only a small surface area is covered by newer rocks, such as psamites, marges and limestone, which are up to 35 million years old.

Naxos is also known for the production of emery, which in the past was even exported abroad. Emery usually appears in marble and is plentiful in the north-east section of the island. It is most probably created by the metamorphosis of bauxite. The use of magnetite as an iron ore is also widespread in Naxos.

1. Exhibition hall in the Geological Collection of Petros Protopapadakis, Apeiranthos.
2. The bay of Abram.
3. Transportation of emery from the quarry to the port.

3

HISTORY

Naxos is and always has been a cross-roads, where archaeologists, historians, scholars of all kinds, artists, and ordinary people with an interest in history, archaeology and folklore can meet, drawn by the importance of the culture which has flourished on the island down the centuries.

Among the archaeologists to have worked on Naxos since the beginning of the 20th century are Professors Welter, Doumas, Lambrinoudakis, Drandrakis, Klon Stefanos, Christos Karouzos, N. Kontoleon, N. Zafiropoulos,

'The ship of Dionysos',
interior of a cup by the Exekias painter, 6th century BC.
This representation has been inspired by tradition and the Homeric Hymn on the capture of Dionysos by Etruscan pirates and the god's ultimate triumph, somewhere in the sea just off Naxos.

on Olympus! The island would seem to have had extensive grazing-grounds in ancient times, and Naxiot animals were so highly thought of that when in the 6th century BC Polycrates, tyrant of Samos, was searching for breeding animals with which to improve his stock, he sent to Naxos for goats

The marble and emery of Naxos were soon in use in art and daily life far beyond the bounds of the island. The myths relating to Naxos reflect its agricultural society, pastoral surroundings and general air of prosperity.

F. Zafiropoulou and G. Gruben, professor of the history of architecture at the University of Munich. and Korres (who is responsible for the restoration of the Athens Acropolis). These scholars have concluded that Naxos was not merely significant but of decisive importance for the history of the Cyclades and of the Greek world in general.

Its size, its central position in the Aegean, the fertility of its soil and the prosperity that these factors created helped to assure Naxos its self-sufficiency down the ages.

Pindar calls Naxos «rich» and Herodotus assures us that Naxos «surpassed the other isles in prosperity.» Just as today, the fruit, olive oil and above all wine of Naxos were famous in antiquity: Archilochus of Paros even went to far as to compare Naxiot wine with the nectar drunk by the gods

Mythology

It is said, for instance, that Zeus himself was raised there, and was worshipped as Zeus Melosios, protector of the flocks.

Apollo, who had a special connection with the island, was also worshipped as the protector of the flocks particularly of the rams and also of flowers.

Ares, god of war, was once forced to take refuge from his pursuers in the depths of the earth of Naxos, where he hid in what the myth calls «the stone that eats iron», an obvious reference to emery.

Above all, though, it was Dionysus who embodied all the bucolic charms and advantages of Naxos. It was here that the god was born and raised, according to the local myth, and all the myths agree that it was on Naxos that he met and married

Thomas Hope: view of Naxos with the Gate of the Temple of Bacchus, ca. 1795, Athens, Benaki Museum.

Ariadne, after she had been abandoned on the island by Theseus. The marriage between Ariadne and Dionysus, her death and the rebirth which that death fore-shadows were the focus of wild celebrations on Naxos in antiquity, where this cult, focusing on the ripening, death and regeneration of nature was most highly developed.

The first inhabitants of Naxos are said by the myths to have been Thracian, under Boutes, son of Boreas (the north wind). In his desire to find wives for his companions, Boutes took the rather extreme step of hunting some Maenads in Thessaly; he captured some, including Coronis and Iphimedeia, and brought them back to the island.

The myths relate that the Thracians held Naxos for two hundred years, being succeeded by Carians from Asia Minor, whose king Naxos gave the island its name. Archaeological finds indicate that there was a fairly well-developed society on Naxos as early as the late 4th millennium BC, about the end of the Neolithic age.

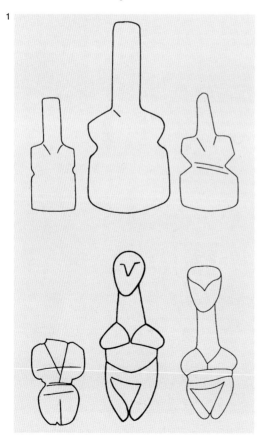

The Cycladic period

The first major flowering of civilisation on Naxos occurred during the 3rd millennium and is known as the Cycladic period, since it spread through all the islands in the group. Naxos at this time had a large population scattered in small settlements most of which were on the steep and less fertile eastern side of the island. The island was under some form of undisputed central control and it seems very likely that Naxos also ruled areas outside its own natural frontiers, particularly to the east and south where a number of islets would have acted as an obvious axis along which to expand. A typical settlement dating from this period has been excavated at the spot called 'Korfari ton Amigdalion,' at Panormos.

Grotta, the site on which the modern town of Naxos (Hora) stands, has yielded evidence of a much larger and more developed settlement in the Cycladic age, with walls and stone houses, square in shape and carefully built. Rich pottery finds have also come to light on the site.

In fact, however, we know much more about the island's cemeteries than we do about its towns. The graves, which have been found all over the island, have yielded masterpieces of art and craftsmanship dating from the second half of the 3rd millennium, and the number and variety of forms discovered on Naxos are greater than for most other Cycladic centres. These finds include clay and marble vessels, metal objects and miniatures, and, above all, the marble figurines so typical of Cycladic art, with their simplicity of form, clarity of line and austerity of style - creations of rare if not unique sensitivity for the prehistoric era.

These figurines are the best example of the Cycladic style of sculpture, the first real sculpture in Greece, even though the scale may be small and unlike the monumental creations to which one is accustomed. Indeed, centuries after the end of the Cycladic civilisation as such, this sculpture was still being produced on Naxos.

1. Drawings of various types of idol.
2. Idol from the Louros cemetery on Naxos
   (Athens, National Archaeological Museum)
3. Marble sculpture of a female figure, Cycladic period
   (2800-2200 BC, Athens, National Archaeological Museum.)

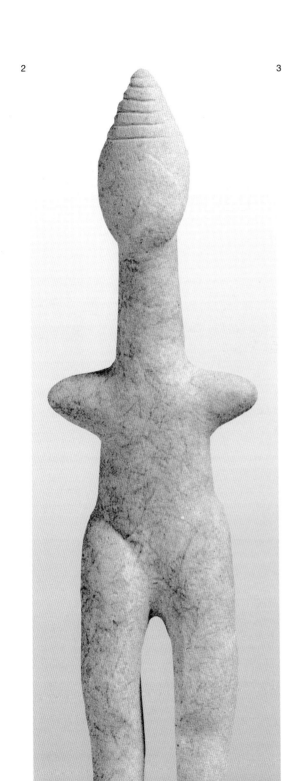

The Mycenean Period

During the course of the 2nd millennium BC the autonomy of the fresh and original civilisation of the Cyclades began to decline in the face of the rising power of other centres in the Aegean: first that of Minoan Crete and later that of Mycenean Greece.

When the Minoan empire collapsed in about 1400 BC the Aegean islands formed a bridge by way of which the power of Mycenae and similar centres was able to expand eastwards.

The population of Naxos moved north-west, in the direction of mainland Greece. It was at this time that the large Mycenean city was founded at Grotta, a settlement which was to survive into the early Geometric period (c. 1000 BC). Huge cemeteries grew up at Aplomata and Kamini.

A myth tells us that the fleet of Neleus, son of Codrus the last king of Athens, was blown off course by a storm while sailing east and landed at Naxos. This is indicative of the island's role as a way-station between Greece and the east and a stopover for Mycenean craft travelling in that direction.

Geometric and Archaic Periods

By about the 7th century BC Naxos had an oligarchic regime with an extensive caste of rich and powerful nobles known as 'pacheis', the fat ones. The main town stood on the hill which the Kastro of Hora now occupies and there were also settlements in other parts of the island. Agriculture and stock-breeding continued to be the chief occupation of the populace, along with fishing, trade and crafts.

Naxos sent colonists to Arkesine and perhaps Aigiale on Anaphi, and close relations grew up with Thira (Santorini). Jumping to a somewhat later period (so as to show the extent of colonisation from Naxos), in 734 BC the island lent its ships to the city of Chalkis, with which it had friendly relations, to send colonists west. They went to Sicily and, in gratitude for having provided the transport, the settlers from Chalkis gave the name of 'Naxos' to one of the colonies that they founded there.

During the Archaic period, Naxos was in continuous conflict with Miletus, Erythrae and Paros. During one of the wars Archilochus of Paros, his

island's greatest poet, was killed. It would appear from the monuments that Naxos in the 7th and early 6th centuries controlled and operated, almost without challenge, the major Ionian religious centre of Delos. The oldest buildings on Delos and many of the most important offerings are Naxiot, and given that Delos was sacred to Apollo, it might be said that the policy of Naxos at this time was 'the Apollo line.'

The deme (community) of Naxiots dedicated a number of valuable vessels to Delian Apollo and also a number of highly impressive monuments to the god's other shrines, notably the Sphinx at Delphi. Naxiot colonists carried the worship of Apollo to Amorgos and during the Archaic period there was a strong Naxiot presence at the shrine of Ptoan Apollo in Boeotia.

This flourishing of the island's society was accompanied from a very early date by the development of the arts. It was on Naxos that the school of sculpture that would leave its mark on all antiquity rose to prominence and took on the element of the monumental.

Marble had always been an abundant and familiar material on Naxos. At about this period it

1. The Lions of Delos, a Naxiot dedication to the god Apollo.
2. The Sphinx, Naxiot dedication to the temple of Apollo at Delphi.

began to be exported for the huge building projects on Delos and the other important Greek sanctuaries wherever man felt the need to express himself in terms rather larger than life. Indeed the craftsmen of Naxos had considerable influence on the exact nature of the finished product, since the statues left their quarries with the rough outlines of their shapes already carved. And it was emery, another Naxiot product, that was used to finish off the work.

Not surprisingly, the craftsmen of Naxos were much sought after, and the fortunes they made allowed them to dedicate expensive offerings of their own to the gods. They were the first people to build entire structures of pure and unalloyed marble, and there is a legend that Byzes and his son Euergos, sculptors and builders, were the first craftsmen to make marble tiles.

The large nude statues of men and clothed statues of women known to be from Naxos are among the earliest of their type found in Greece. Among the best-known examples is the Artemis (c. 650 BC) dedicated by Nikandra of Naxos, a member of one of the island's wealthy families, and found on Delos. It can be seen in the National Archaeolo-

gical Museum in Athens. Kouroi of the third quarter of the 7th century made their way from Naxos to Thira, to be unearthed in archaeological excavations. The marble Apollo raised on Delos by the Naxiots about 600 BC was nearly 25 feet tall.

Among other imposing examples of Naxiot work are the enormous lions also to be seen on Delos. But the most impressive pieces of all are those that were never finished. They are to be seen at various places on Naxos or even in the quarries where they were being produced. Two of these kouroi are at Melyes, while the statue of Dionysus at Apollonas is more than 30 feet tall. It seems that, apart from the practical difficulty of moving these monsters, there may well have been other reasons -perhaps the death of the client or political upheaval- which led to their being abandoned.

Whole buildings also fell within the scope of the Naxiot craftsmen, and the 'House of the Naxiots' on Delos, dating from the late 7th century, was the most important edifice of its time on the sacred island. At home, the marble temple on the islet of Palatia was in antiquity, and still is today, a sort of 'trademark' for Naxos.

Archaeological research is still uncovering hitherto unknown aspects of the island's past. Just how interesting and important was the temple to Demeter at Gyroulas, near Sangri, has only recently been revealed. The various parts of the temple, including its marble roof, have survived in such good condition that it would even be possible to reerect it. It would be possible, that is, for Naxos to acquire a monument of unique significance for Ionian art, equivalent to the temple of Aphaia on Aegina in the Saronic. And as recently as the summer of 1986 a particularly large temple (13.5 metres by 25 metres) came to light at Iria. This temple was built in the mid-6th century and functioned for nine consecutive centuries until its violent destruction in the 3rd century AD. This find is of great importance for the history of Greek architecture because the temple was built at a time when the transition from granite to marble was being made. Political turmoil, though, was also a feature of this period in Naxiot history. When, for instance, the widely-respected nobleman Telestagoras was insulted by others of his class, popular feeling against the wealthy broke out into action. The chaos was exploited by another noble, Lygdamis, who with the help of his friend the tyrant Peisistratus of Athens, took control of Naxos in about 540 BC and installed his own tyranny. It lasted until 524 BC, when Lygdamis was overthrown by the Spartans. After a brief period of oligarchy, democracy returned to Naxos, and the island was able to withstand a four-month siege by Aristagoras, tyrant of Miletus, in 506 BC.

The classical period

For some reason the Naxiots adopted a passive stance when the Persians attacked Greece in 490 BC. Most of the populace took refuge in the mountains; those who remained in the city were enslaved, and the city itself was burned and its temples destroyed. Yet at the battle of Salamis the Naxiot conscripts deserted their Persian masters and took the Athenian side. Many Naxiots fought at the battle of Plataea, and the island's name was on the roll of honour inscribed on the tripod at Delphi and on the base of a statue of Zeus at Olympia. Even so, the destruction of Naxos by the Persians effectively marked the end of the island's independent history. At the end of the Persian wars, it came under Athenian control and all efforts to escape from it proved fruitless until the defeat of Athens by Sparta in the Peloponnesian War. Spartan dominance did not bring peace, though, and in the 4th century the Athenians and Spartans were to fight over Naxos again. Naxos later joined the 'League of Islanders' and came under the influence first of the Ptolemies of Egypt, then of Macedon and finally of Rhodes. After 41 BC Naxos formed part of the Roman eparchy of the islands whose headquarters was in Rhodes an administrative arrangement mirrored, in the early Christian era, by the subjection of the church in Naxos to episcopal control from Rhodes.The Romans also used the island as a place of exile.

Byzantium - Venetian rule and Turkish conquest

The Byzantine period has left clear marks on Naxos: some five hundred churches and

monasteries of all possible styles and types, with excellent wall-paintings, icons, friezes, inscriptions and so on. Early Christian churches have been built on the remains of ancient temples, and during the iconoclastic period churches on Naxos were decorated without the use of icons. Caves thought in ancient times to be the haunts of nymphs and gods were also converted into Christian shrines, and when the pirates began to ravage the islands, the monasteries were fortified to keep them out.

It is believed by many scholars that in Byzantine times the centres of life on Naxos were in the Tragaia-Apano Kastro and Sangri-Kastro t'Apalirou regions (as far as Ayiasos Bay).

The plain of Sangri, with its scores of little churches, has been described as a smaller version of Mystras in the Peloponnese. Inscriptions have revealed that before 1080 Naxos was the seat of the provincial governor controlling one third of the 'theme' - administrative unit - of the Aegean, named Nikitas, and of other senior officials. Naxos was the see of a bishop and, after 1088, of a metropolitan bishop. On a local and provincial level at least, Naxos must have been quite an important place during the Byzantine period. In 1207 (only three years after the fall of Byzantium to Western raiders) Marco Sanudo of Venice captured the Cyclades and set up the Duchy of Naxos, otherwise known as the Duchy of the Aegean, with Naxos as its headquarters. It would seem that Sanudo landed on Naxos at Ayiasos and captured the Kastro t' Apalirou (the Byzantine centre of the island) after a 40-day resistance by the islanders. Sanudo went on to build his own castle, the Kastro, at Hora on the site of the ancient acropolis. He divided Naxos into 56 estates, which he shared out among his officers. They in turn built their own fortresses on the most suitable site of each estate.

The Duchy of Naxos continued to be a considerable power for over three hundred years, until 1564. In that year Naxos came under Turkish rule, but the reins of power continued to be held by the Venetians, given that the only interest the Ottoman Empire displayed was in collecting its taxes once a year.

1. Kastro t'Apalirou at Tragaia.
2. The church of Ayii Apostoloi at Tragaia.
3. The church of Ayios Ioannis the Diasoritis, Halkis.

Very few Turks settled on Naxos, particularly after the 17th century. Those who did settle lived with the constant fear of the Greek and Western pirates who infested the area and preyed exclusively on Turks. This terror of capture and slaughter led the Turks of Naxos to sell up and move out, and so when the War of Independence started in 1821 the only Turk on the island was a clerk, who sailed away in a little boat as soon as the first vague rumours of an uprising reached the island. The centuries of Turkish rule on Naxos have thus left very few traces; a few place names, and a ruined fountain, the 'Aga's fountain', on the road from Hora to Engares. It was built by Hasan Aga, «glorious voivode of Naxos» on 26 June 1759 to ensure himself of the eternal gratitude of thirsty travellers. The period of Turkish rule was a fruitful one for the building of churches and schools, such as the Monasteries of Panayia (Our Lady) Faneromeni and

of Ayios Chrysostomos, the cathedral church in Hora and the church of Ayia Kyriaki, the Ayios Georgios Grotta school in Hora (where Chrysanthos of Aetolia, brother of the 18th-century missionary Kosmas the Aetolian, was among the teachers), of Ayios Eleutherios at Sangri, the Ursuline School and the Commercial School in the Kastro. The islanders of Naxos often rose in rebellion against their Venetian and Turkish overlords. In August 1595, for instance, a daring plot to throw off the Turkish yoke was hatched on Naxos by representatives of fifteen islands. There were further uprisings in 1563, 1643, 1670 and 1681, but the most important were those of the 18th century. These uprisings centred around the Politis family and their fortified house at Akadimi in the plain of Tragaia (a building which today belongs to the Papadakis family). Markakis Politis, builder of the house and leader of the 'Community of Villages,' fought the conquerors constantly from 1770 to 1802. He was the terror of the Venetians and the idol of the Greeks.

Independence

In order to keep a watch over the feudal Varotsis clan of Drymalia, who ruled Halki and Filoti, Markakis Politis built his tower at Akadimi, facing the tower of Bernardo Varotsis. From this stronghold he organised the peasants of Drymalia against their feudal overlord.

Politis did not hesitate to make use of the Turks in his struggle against Varotsis. Given that the Turks were interested primarily in getting their taxes, Politis made sure he always paid up on time, and so he gained their respect and trust. He contributed to the running of the Ayios Georgos School at Grotta, and has been called the «resurrection of Naxos» and «protagonist in the ending of feudalism.» The Venetian families, naturally enough, persecuted and slandered him, and he was eventually exiled to Mytilene. Here, he met his end on 25 March 1802, strangled with a rope on the orders of Pasha Kunguhi Hussein, pasha of the islands.

Markakis Politis' son was known as Michalakis Markopolitis, and he carried on his father's work. He was pronounced leader of the Community of Villages and fought against both Venetians and Turks.

When the War of Independence broke out in 1821, Markopolitis took an active role, representing Naxos at the General Assemblies which were free Greece's first parliaments. In 1851 he was appointed Senator.

Alexandros Ipsilantis, one of the leaders of the liberation struggle, had sent his men into the Cyclades with news of the coming rising as early as late 1820. In December of that year the Society of Friends, the organisation which sponsored the rebellion, enrolled its first members on Naxos, among them Markopolitis. The island's independence was declared on 6 May 1821.

1. One of the coats of arms from above the entrances to the Frankish mansions.
2. 'The garrison of Naxos,' engraving by André Gruret Saint-Souveuer, Gennadios Library, Athens.

CULTURE & TRADITION

People and Occupations

The inhabitants of Naxos are friendly and open-hearted. Hospitable and affable, they immediately make a good impression on all those who visit the island. They have a great reputation for their love of their island, their traditions and customs. Even during the period when for many migration appeared to be the only way of ensuring a better future, those Naxiots far from their island never stopped living for and dreaming of the day of their return. There were many reasons for migrating. Naxos is a small island, an isolated provincial region, and a link in one of the prefectures of Greece that has the most problems.

And yet, in contrast with most of the islands, to quote the local 'Aigaion' newspaper of 1905:

«Our island is a place of agriculture, a place of stock breeding, a place with all the benefits of a fortunate and happy isle. Cheese, stock, grain, potatoes, onions, citrus fruit, other fruit of every nature provide the means of trade throughout the year...»

The Naxiots, then, have always cultivated their land with care, they have delved to its depths to extract its emery and have always been masters of their mountains, where they have guarded their flocks. The island has always been marked by its self-sufficiency.

It is exactly for this reason that the people of Naxos have never turned towards the sea. The largest island of the Cyclades can boast very few sea-captains, a dozen at the most. Here, of course, we are not speaking of the simple fishermen, whose experience and daring served in the relaying of messages and the hiding of fighters during the Resistance of World War II.

The proverbs of the Naxiots reveal the islander's relationship with nature and reflect the variety of his occupations - most of which have to do with the life of the farmer and shepherd and very few with the sea.

Some proverbs, which are still said in Naxos today, are:

If all the bees made honey,
there would be enough for even the gypsies to eat.

The meaning of this is that every job requires certain abilities, which are not possessed by all

The mill needs a miller and the ship a wind, as a girl needs
a warm embrace as rosy dawn steals nigh.

This is taken to mean that every occupation needs the right person.

Sorting the figs can leave you with none at all.

When someone sets out to make a selection, he ends up by rejecting nothing.

If the ox knew his own strength. God help us.

This is applied to people who are not aware of their own potential.

Throw stones at the walnut-trees, but not at the maple.

The meaning here is that people speak ill of those who are worth slandering, not of nonentities. The walnut-tree bears nuts and so stones are thrown at it to dislodge them; the maple bears nothing of use, so why throw stones at it?

A goat thief came along and they put him in jail;
when a real scoundrel turned up,
they took off their hats to him.

The poor, that is, pay the penalty, while the powerful are held in esteem, even when they are criminals. This proverb also reminds us that in upland Naxos, particularly in the largely agricultural Apeiranthos area, 'rustling' was a common phenomenon. Animal theft was thought of more as a custom than as an infringement of the Penal Code. In other words, it was a typical feature of an 'archaic society,' such as that of Apeiranthos, where ancient practices were kept up and where the goat thieves were 'palikaria', heroic young men. Those who ran the risk of stealing animals far from their own village were revered as being particularly brave. The self-sufficiency of a small island is, of course, fragile, and such islands are unlikely to be able to meet all the needs of their inhabitants, especially those who live in mountain communities. Thus the Naxiots often went to seek their fortune elsewhere, to places such as Smyrna, Constantinople, Canada and the United States.

These emigrants provided those who stayed at home with valuable financial support and also enlarged their fund of experience of the world. Stories of marvellous and 'modern' songs and dances filled the island, but did not displace its own tradition.

Weaving

Naxos is still celebrated for its textiles.

«I sit here at my loom and weave
And find out what you're doing;
Ill-wishers come and tell me all
About your ways in wooing.

I hear your treadle rise and fall
The bobbins whirl and scuttle,
But you, my girl, are worthy of
A diamond-studded shuttle,

Come, up you get, you weaver maid
Go out and look on high
And see the stars as they shine forth
Across the midnight sky..».

These 'kotsakia' serve to remind us of the relationship of the women of Naxos with the loom and the value of their creations, a value which is not only aesthetic but also functional.

Naxos has an important weaving tradition, as it does in needlework, although Naxos textiles are not particularly well-known in the rest of Greece.

At Apeiranthos and Moni, the chief centres for this craft, every house has its own loom (called krevataria locally). It was always considered praiseworthy for a woman to be a weaver; this is because what they wove was far from being purely decorative. First and foremost, they wove all the clothes for their families, from the shirts of the emery-workers to a kind of hooded coat for babies. They wove shoulder bags, curtains, the surrounds for the old-style bed, covers for the traditional island settle, cushion covers, mats, tablecloths and kerchief holders.

Thus the women, by the labours of their own hands, clothed their families, decorated their homes and amassed their daughters' dowry.

Each item was a genuine creation, made with love and dreams, and for that reason, though it started off from some basic pattern, there evolved on the loom an endless variety of designs, permutations and colours.

Naxiot textile from the Folk Museum
at Apeiranthos.

Today Naxiot textiles can be seen chiefly at Apeiranthos and Moni. Here there may be an opportunity to purchase some, as there is no systematic market in textiles (with the exception of certain shops in Hora). This is largely because, up to today even, the majority of the women who weave have regarded their work as a purely personal creation, not something for sale.

Naxiot customs

Generally speaking, every day, every season, every feast day is associated with certain special observances which are deeply rooted in the past, reflecting the ancient farming and stock-rearing way of life. Many of these are also paralleled in the rest of Greece. Here we will confine ourselves to mentioning some customs which are special to Naxos and which truly continue to 'live' today.

Carnival: the 'Bell-wearers'

In the mountain villages (Apeiranthos, Filoti) certain features of the ancient Dionysiac cult still survive. In addition to the fancy dress known everywhere, in the period just before the beginning of Lent the 'bell-wearers' make their appearance. These are young men who wear the so-called 'abadelli' a cloak with a hood, and have their faces covered with silk or muslin scarves to conceal their identity. A thick rope is wound round their chest and waist, from which hang rows of bells. In their right hand they hold a thick elder stick, called a 'soba.'

The bell-wearers, running from house to house and leaping on to the roofs, make a diabolical noise with their bells and indeed the object is to make as much noise as possible. The bell-wearers strike passers-by with their 'soba' and escort the 'old woman, who is really a man dressed up as an old woman.' She' holds a distaff and a basket to receive the eggs which 'she' collects from the houses that 'she' visits with the bell-wearers. One of the group, dressed in sheep skins and with a large goat bell ('bouka') hung around his neck, pretends to be a bear. Someone else plays the part of his keeper, who leads the bear around and plays a drum for him to dance.

On the last Sunday before the beginning of Lent, the 'paliomoskari' make their appearance without bells, but with blackened faces and dressed in old clothes. They tease the people and are themselves teased in satirical couplets.

On the first day of Lent ('Clean Monday') many people put on the traditional Greek kilt, the 'foustanella,' ribbons of various colours and gold coins. Masks are not worn on this occasion.

On the Saturday preceding the first Sunday of Carnival and on the second Monday it is the custom to slaughter the home-fed pigs. In the old days, villagers competed with each other in producing the fattest pig. The pig-killing was a real holiday: friends and relatives gathered in the yards of the houses and entertained, drank and enjoyed themselves whilst the meat of the pig was being prepared. This included making the renowned 'jamboni' and 'glinero.' The jamboni served all the year round as the most tasty appetiser for friends who dropped in, and the workers in the emery mines would take the cured pork to work with them. Glinero was a kind of lard made from the pig fat. We will see just how much daily needs were 'leavened' with merry-making and festivity.

The 'klidonas'

On the evening of 23 June the custom is to light the bonfires of Ayios Ioannis, St John, and to burn thistles. From the ashes that remain, the girls will discover the next morning whom they will marry.

On this day, the young men and women must go to three wells to fetch the 'silent water' (collected without speaking). On their return they pass a cross-roads where three roads, three alleyways and three churches meet. They must then take the water home, mix it with equal quantities of flour and salt and cook and eat the resultant 'salty pies.' They will then have sweet dreams of the one they love giving them water to drink.

The making of wine and raki

«We're making wine,
So come and help,
Stand in the vat
And tread the grape,

And if our grapes are trodden
By one as sweet as you,
Then this year's wine will surely be
As sweet as honeydew.»

This free translation of the Apeiranthos 'kotsakia' (couplets, see below) illustrates how much the harvesting and treading of the grapes is a festivity, an occasion for communication and high spirits. Less well-known than the grape harvest is the hatzanemata, the work which follows the treading of the grapes and produces raki (also known as 'tsipouro').

When grape treading has finished, what is left in the vat is not thrown away but put into a special vessel, the 'harani,' where it is boiled. The end product of this distillation process is raki.

Naturally, this job also provides an opportunity for relatives and friends to gather together for song, food and wine. It is one of the customs on this occasion to serve aromatic quinces baked in the ashes of the fire which burns under the harani.

3. The production of raki, known as 'hadzanemata,' always provided an opportunity for festivities.

3

1. The Easter Carnival custom of the 'Koudounatoi' has its roots in the ancient worship of Dionysos.
2. Procession with the icon in a Naxiot village.

Easter - the 'patouda'

The great majority of Naxiots, even if they are in the city at Easter, take care to prepare the traditional paschal lamb with 'patouda'. Patouda is a stuffing for the lamb consisting of particular vegetables, lettuce, rice, eggs, currants, the offal of the lamb, large quantities of cheese and fennel - all of which give it a unique aroma and taste.

In the mountain villages of Naxos the lamb was cooked slowly, for hours on end, in a large earthenware bowl in the old ovens fuelled with wood. This no longer happens and, in spite of the unique flavour of patouda, we have lost something of the savour of this dish

Local cuisine

The cuisine of Naxos does not differ much from that of the other Cycladic islands or the rest of Greece. There are, however, a few traditional dishes that it is worth trying, some of which are available in the restaurants.

One of these dishes is 'patouda,' the traditional festive dish that decorates the Easter table. Other traditional specialities of the island are wild rabbit, partridge, 'kalogeros' (a dish with aubergines) and 'kefalopodi' ('head and feet,' a local tripe soup from Apeiranthos).

Naxiot cuisine is also famed for its quality cheeses, fresh vegetables, sweet wines and, of course, the wonderful fresh fish that can be enjoyed at the island's many quaint seaside tavernas.

Songs - Music - Dances

The folk song remains a living feature of life in Naxos today. It could be said that the folk songs of Naxos are famous throughout Greece and have even become fashionable.

It is indicative that whole families of musicians and singers, the Konitopoulos and, the Hadjopoulos families, for example, are Naxiots, as is the fact that the majority of 'island' songs sung by such popular performers as Yannis Parios and Mariza Koch are from Naxos. Naturally, such great popularity and repetition has tended to rob these songs of their original style.

The real Naxiot songs, the Apeiranthos 'kotsakia' mentioned above, are iambic or trochaic couplets with eight-syllable lines (though they can sometimes be of five, six or seven syllables) which always have roughly rhyming endings. Each couplet is usually independent of the others and expresses a complete idea. In their kotsakia ,the people of Apeiranthos give lively but subtle expression to the purity and beauty of love, praise the merits of their beloved, give wishes and advice, condemn infidelity, profess indifference over being deserted and the end of a love affair and give voice to the upheaval caused by the passion of love.

Oh, you have made me lose my mind
And babble in the street;
My love is such that I dissolve
Whene'er we chance to meet,

Patouda

Ingredients: one small whole kid goat, including its entrails, half a kilo of beet, two lettuces, rice, at least eight eggs, raisins, fennel, plenty of cheese (preferably kefalotiri or Naxiot gruyere).

Quickly fry the entrails, chop them into small pieces and bake them with onions and garlic. Cook the vegetables. Boil the eggs and chop them into small pieces. Mix the entrails with the vegetables, eggs, fennel, cheese, raisins and around half a kilo of rice. Fill the chest and stomach of the goat with this mixture and then sew it up. Sprinkle it with lemon, salt and pepper, olive oil and cook over a low flame.

Enjoy your meal!

«The garden flower has promisedme
To bring me for my own

The mountain flower whose form I love
And makes me sigh and moan.»

The majority of the people of Apeiranthos, both men and women, compose their rhyming couplets for every occasion, in times of joy and sadness. They are either sung immediately or written down and sent to friends or relatives who have left the island.

Frequently, when they are dancing and singing, a dialogue develops among the participants, in which everyone seeks to demonstrate their poetic gifts and quick wits. These dialogues are a continuation of poetic contests between men or between young men and women before an audience, which Martin Crusius (Kraus) records as having been held on the island in the 16th century. Of course, the bucolic poet Theocritus also speaks of poetry competitions among simple country people in ancient times. The similarity between the poetic dialogues of Apeiranthos and those of the shepherds in Theocritus permits us to suppose that skill in verse composition at Apeiranthos goes back to very ancient times - at it does in Cyprus, Crete and the Pontus region - and has been handed down as a heritage from one generation to the next.

Apart from the kotsakia, the people of Apeiranthos used to compose, and still do, couplets consisting of iambic 15-syllable rhyming lines, with a wide range of subject matter. There are laudatory poems, rimes, that is satirical narrative songs, dirges, lullabies, carnival songs, wedding songs, carols, songs of exile and songs about the victors in parliamentary or local elections. Some songs are sung by carousers outside the houses of friends and relatives and some are sung under the window of the beloved after midnight. They are frequently accompanied by bagpipe and drum or violin and lute.

The courtyards, the roof tops and the squares of the island continue to be enlivened by songs and dances, such as the balo, the syrtos and the vlacha. Worth noting are two dances from Komiaki; one is called the Vitzilaiadistikos -a dance for large numbers of men at carnival time, to the accompaniment of the bagpipe- and the other Nikintres, the steps of which are the same as those of the syrtos. It is possible to witness such merrymaking, of course.

Old Naxiot costumes (made by N. Katsouros from I. Dellaroca's collection of old designs).

The ancient bucolic poet Theocritus also speaks of summer festivals, of which today there are a large number. One may also have the good fortune to be present at a spontaneous gathering, at Kinidaros, at Apeiranthos, at Danakos, at Koronos, where they will really be initiated into the traditional Naxiot celebration.

Naxos' most important festivals are:
- Zoodochou Pigis at Agrokiliotissa.
- Ayia Triada at Galanado.
- Ayios Georgios at Kinidaro.
- Ayios Nikodemos at Hora.
- Sotiros ('the Saviour') at Damariona, Glinado and Hora.
- Panayia at Filoti and Apeiranthos.
- Stavroproskyniseos at Keramoti.

Art and Literature

Naxos is particularly noted for its 'output' of scientists from as early as the 19th century. As such, not only did this small region literally 'nurture' the whole of Greece with brilliant and distinguished scientists of all specialities, but many of them also achieved high academic positions. Furthermore, Naxos gave birth to three politicians: Petros Protopapadakis, prime minister in 1922 after the tragic end to the Goudi uprising, Aristeides Protopapadakis, Minister of Co-ordination and Defence in the post-war years and Manolis Glezos, the First Partisan of Europe and one of the most significant figures to have emerged from the Greek Left.

The vibrant cultural creativity of the Naxiots is also witnessed in the publishing activity of the island, especially during the nineteenth century. The appearance of the first printing press on the island is dated to around 1890 and the first Naxiot newspaper, 'Naxos,' was published in 1894 at the island's printing press. Other newspapers followed, but a major event in Naxiot newspaper production was the launch of the 'Aigaion' in 1902, a newspaper which is still going strong today.

It writes: «The purpose of journalism is not to inform about comings and goings, nor the placing of flamboyant advertisements for various shops».

It has taken an interest in all the issues that affect Naxos even today, as, of course, has the whole of the Naxiot press, which includes ten publications.

Self-sufficiency and the involvement of the Naxiots in cultural activities has meant that it is only recently that they have become particularly involved with tourism.

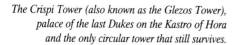

The Crispi Tower (also known as the Glezos Tower), palace of the last Dukes on the Kastro of Hora and the only circular tower that still survives.

40

Architecture

The architecture of Naxos followed the historical events of the island and responded each time to the requirements of the historical conditions.

In the early years of the Byzantine Empire the residents of the island lived on the coasts and most of them were centred around the port of Ayiasos. In the later Byzantine period, with the start of the pirate raids, settlements grew up in the interior of the island. The Naxiots built garrisons near these settlements, which they would lock themselves into in order to fight the raiders.

Later, in 1207, when Frankish rule under Marco Sanudo was set up on the island, a castle with towers around it was built on the island - a symbol of secular and ecclesiastical power - in order to establish the Frankish leader's position. The old towers were given to his associates; some of these were repaired whilst some new towers were also built.

The Kastro (castle) in the Hora - the main town - of Naxos was built according to a plan that detailed precisely how the garrison would be built and what the relationship between the provision of housing and the defence wall was to be. According to accounts, the defence wall was in the form of a pentagon with five towers at each point. There was a triangular area in the direction of the port and a rectangular area towards the hinterland. Another account says that there were twelve towers, at a distance of ten metres apart, whilst the part of the wall with the houses was closed off by three gates that were in three of the points of the pentagonal wall. Today, the gate in Prantouna Square and the north-west gate next to the only-surviving tower, Glezos' Tower, are still standing. Only one section of this tower, which was originally very tall, survives. The entrances to the houses in the perimeter walls are inside of the Kastro and overlook a peripheral road. There are other houses with the same circumference as those in the

peripheral wall which must have been built at a later date.

There are many roads with steps leading out from the inner peripheral road; these roads follow the natural morphology of the land and lead into the main square of the Kastro.

The Kastro of Naxos is one of the few settlements in Greece with the layout of a medieval town to survive as a whole. It bears the symbols of ecclesiastical and secular power at its centre, that is the Catholic cathedral and a central tower. The monasteries of St Anthony and of the Capuchin, the Ursuline Convent, where Catholic girls of the island were educated, and the School of Commerce, in which Catholic monks taught, are buildings within the Kastro that show the attempt made by the Venetians to transmit the western mode of thought, with religion as its main form of expression. The Duke's vassals lived outside the Kastro, along with the inhabitants of the island, establishing the districts of Bourgos and Agora. The villages of Grotta and Fontana were founded later by Jews who came to the island and the village of Nio Horio by Cretans and refugees from Asia Minor.

The houses of Naxos can be divided into three categories:
a) mansions,
b) popular housing, and
c) the towers.

43

Mansions

The mansions are mainly to be found within the Kastro and had garrison features. There are also other types of mansion that do not share these features and which belonged to rich merchants. One might say that the mansions were the houses of the Cycladic bourgeoisie. Their layout does not appear to have evolved from any other type of Cycladic house. They have one central sitting room with rooms of equal size around it. The seating area is distinct and allows the whole family to congregate within it. The function of the courtyard is substituted for by the sitting room. Due to their position, the mansions on the periphery of the Kastro have a fortress-like character, especially in the basements, although this is less apparent on the ground floors and pretty much disappears in the upper floors. There are small rooms on the upper floor, in the case where one exists, and these mansions are reminiscent of the popular housing. Large rooms, tall main areas, low basements, thick walls - these are some of the characteristics of the mansions of the Kastro.

Popular housing

The popular house is the most common form of housing on Naxos. It was originally limited to a one-roomed dwelling, which covered the needs only of shelter and the storage of goods. These houses later came to include spaces with different uses, such as the living room for sleeping and day-time use, which was divided into two areas of equal size; a separate kitchen which was also used as a dining room; a chicken coop and a courtyard around which all the other areas were centred. This outside area was an indispensable part of the house, and it was in direct and daily communication with the living room and the kitchen. In some cases another floor was added, thus creating a new type of house, the 'anokatogo' ('the upstairs-downstairs'), which is found mainly in the Hora. This type of house was particularly widespread, something which can be easily explained by the dense population and the sloping terrain.

There was no one shape for the layout of the houses, but they were mainly rectangular. In many instances there was one room that distorted this shape, being located above the road or above the neighbouring house. The houses were built next to each other whilst the courtyards were very small. The various household functions were performed in the 'katoï' (ground floor) area: the kitchen, the cellar or storehouse and the toilet. The living room was rarely situated on the ground floor but very often there was a dining room next to the kitchen. The kitchen was a very important part of the house. The fireplace for cooking, the sink, the sideboard, with small recesses and cupboards in the walls, the dresser-these are all features that were necessary for the proper functioning of the kitchen. The kitchen was long and narrow with the fireplace taking up one whole wall. The main feature of the 'anoï' (upper floor) was the sitting room, which took up the largest and most central portion of the house, perhaps the only space which exuded a sense of luxury in contrast with the austerity of the rest of the house. Next to the sitting room were the other rooms, the bedrooms being very small, whilst the anoï communicated with the katoï via an internal staircase. The absence of many hallways and the simplification, as far as it was possible, of the operational functions of the house are characteristic features. The existence of an outside area, which came in many different shapes, was also characteristic.

1

Typical features of the Naxiot house - the large reception room and living room on the upper floor, the storage areas and the auxiliary rooms on the lower floor - are all retained in the towers, the difference being that they are spread over more floors. The lower floor, the 'katoï,' is taken up entirely by the auxiliary rooms, which are large in size, and storage-rooms for foodstuffs. The harvests were stored in these, especially during periods of drought and the long sieges. Communication between the katoï and the upper floor was via a hatch-door and a wooden or stone staircase from the outside whilst inside the tower there was a stone staircase which led to the balcony of the first floor, where the main entrance to the tower was.

It is also interesting to note that in some towers the stairway did not go all the way up to the entrance but stopped a fair distance below. Access was then continued via a wooden platform or bridge which was raised whenever raiders threatened the security of the building.

Western influence is mainly noticeable in the layout, which now followed the pre-determined plan of an enclosed rectangle with symmetrical lines of axis. The design of the entrance to the tower is now especially formal and the western element is especially highlighted in features such as the ramparts from which boiling oil was poured. The geometric schema is made especially pronounced by the lack of atypical extensions and the façades were not whitewashed, something that would have provided a sense of lightness and joy. In general, all the towers have either the colour of the stone or the earth and bond harmonically with the natural environment. An experienced eye can trace a sense of symmetry along the width and the height. The only decorative elements are the windows and doors

Towers

There are around thirty towers still surviving in Naxos, most of which were built by the Venetians after 1600 in order to fortify the island against pirate raids but also to impose their rule onto the locals. There are also monastery-towers built by the locals in order to defend their rights against the Venetians. Both types of tower have a defensive character. There are also some towers that were used by the Venetians as country residences, which do not have a defensive character.

Each tower is surrounded by a wall that encloses the courtyard and the auxiliary buildings. Large storage areas were also needed in order to store the fruits of Naxos' rich, fertile earth and also for use as stables.

There was often a wine-press in the auxiliary buildings. As these towers were intended to house the Frankish conquerors one might expect that they would be built in a western style. The fact, however, that they were built by local artisans resulted in a mixture of Cycladic and western architecture, and this is especially apparent in the layout.

Note: the details on the architecture of Naxos have been taken from the book 'Greek Traditional Architecture': Naxos (Melissa publications), Athens 1982.

1. The Cheimarros Tower.
2. The Zevgolis Tower with its coat of arms.
3. The Belonias Tower.

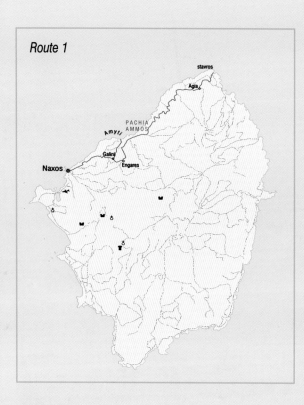

Route 1

Route 2

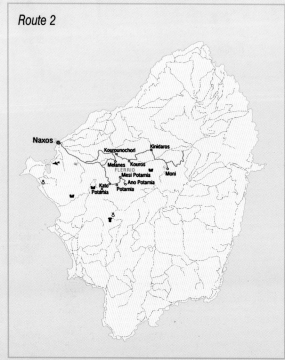

Route 3

NAXOS

Don't forget to see...

Route 4

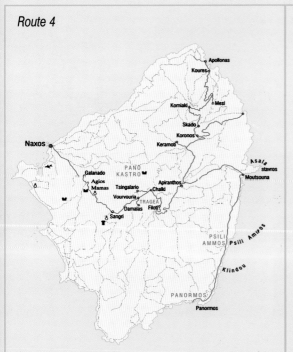

Route 5
Getting to know Zas

HORA (The town of Naxos)

The islet of Palatia

The first walk which we should mention is the traditional stroll at the Palatia or Portara, also known as the Baths of Ariadne. This is the huge marble gate, the Portara, on the islet in front of the harbour that captures your eye as soon as you arrive in Naxos.

We known that during the period between antiquity and today the level of the Mediterranean Sea has risen significantly. Consequently, the low-lying parts of what were coastal areas in ancient times are now covered by the sea. It would seem, then, that the Palatia islet was once a hill, lower than that of the 'Kastro,' which rose from a more extensive coastal plain. In the 3rd millennium BC there was a settlement near the islet and it is conjectured that the Palatia was the acropolis of this Cycladic village. The area was subsequently deserted for many centuries. All we can see today are the foundations and the huge portal of the 'hundred-foot' temple begun around 530 BC by Lygdamis, tyrant of Naxos, but never completed.

The 'Portara' was built with four blocks of marble, each over 6 metres long and weighing 20 tons. Winches and scaffolding were used to put them in place.

The threshold of the portal is higher than the floor of the temple, a phenomenon who occurs elsewhere only in the case of the temple of 'Twin' Apollo at Miletus. The temple was planned to be rectangular with pillars on the two short sides. The Portara exactly faces Delos and this is seen as a reference to Apollo, the temple being identified as the Delion (temple of Delian Apollo), although some scholars associate it with Dionysus, on the grounds that Naxos was the birthplace of Bacchus and the island where Theseus left Ariadne inconsolable, until she obtained the protection of Dionysus. In the 6th century BC the Palatia served as a good stronghold near the town and it was there, it seems that the Erythreans and the Milesians based themselves in one of their attacks on Naxos. However, a noble Naxiot lady, Polycrite, whom the leader of the Erythreans had fallen in love with and carried off,

helped to save Naxos. She sent a message from the enemy camp to her brothers, informing them of the day on which the enemy would celebrate the Thargelia (a festival in honour of Apollo) by baking a lead tablet in a loaf of bread. The Palatia temple was converted into a Christian church in the 5th or 6th century AD. Under Frankish rule a great deal of marble was taken for building works in the Kastro area. This destruction continued under the Turks, with the result that only the foundations remained, together with the 'Portara,' which was so big that they did not have the means to demolish it.

Aside from its historical and archaeological significance, the little island of Palatia is a unique point in the Aegean Sea, from which you can soak up the sunset and look out over Paros, Delos, Mykonos and Syros in the distance, whenever the horizon is clear. And as you do so, you will remember the words of Georgios Theotokas: «A small boat which goes fishing in between Paros and Naxos interests me incomparably far more than a new revolution, a new fashion or aesthetic trend from Europe, a new machine from America or a new form of

mysticism from Asia. Serenity! Serenity!»

The little island of Palatia is physically linked to Grotta, Aplomata and Kaminaki.

Grotta is Hora's northern coast and took its name from the caves beneath the hill of Aplomata, i.e. from the hill just past Grotta, into which the sea enters quite deeply. Nevertheless, earthquakes, subsidence and, of course, the rising sea level, have changed the appearance of the area from antiquity until today. The Mycenean city of Naxos was in the area of Grotta. This was one of the most important, if not the most important, Mycenean cities of the Aegean. The buildings even extend into the sea. It is believed that the Mycenean acropolis was located on the top of the Kastro. The large cemeteries of the period were at Aplomata and, further east, at Kamini.

The town and region of Grotta
(view from Portara).

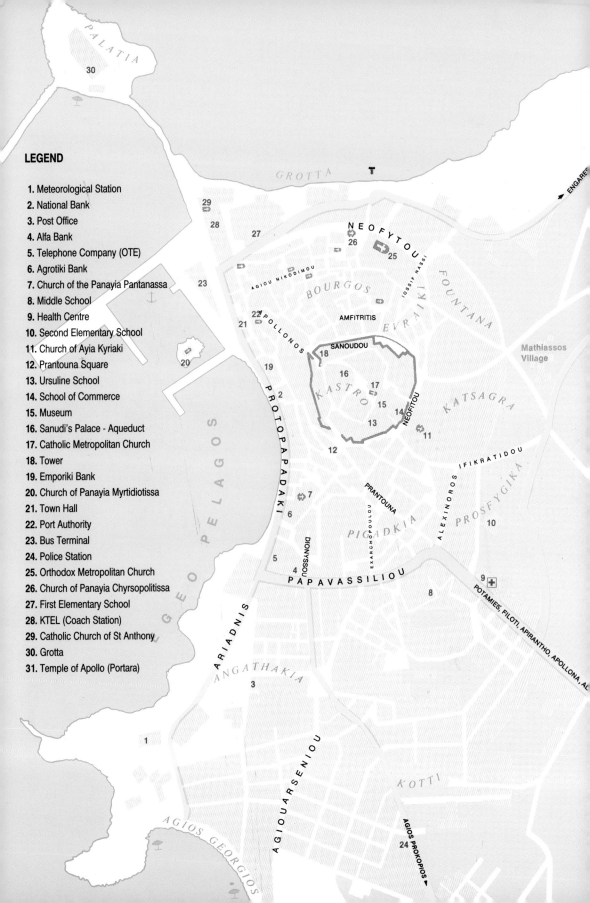

LEGEND

1. Meteorological Station
2. National Bank
3. Post Office
4. Alfa Bank
5. Telephone Company (OTE)
6. Agrotiki Bank
7. Church of the Panayia Pantanassa
8. Middle School
9. Health Centre
10. Second Elementary School
11. Church of Ayia Kyriaki
12. Prantouna Square
13. Ursuline School
14. School of Commerce
15. Museum
16. Sanudi's Palace - Aqueduct
17. Catholic Metropolitan Church
18. Tower
19. Emporiki Bank
20. Church of Panayia Myrtidiotissa
21. Town Hall
22. Port Authority
23. Bus Terminal
24. Police Station
25. Orthodox Metropolitan Church
26. Church of Panayia Chyrsopolitissa
27. First Elementary School
28. KTEL (Coach Station)
29. Catholic Church of St Anthony
30. Grotta
31. Temple of Apollo (Portara)

Hora and the little church of Panayia Myrtidiotissa.

Old Hora - Kastro

The narrow covered streets, with their unexpected dead ends, twists and turns, steps, deadlights, corbels and balconies suggest that the only thought in the minds of the people who laid out this town was defence against an enemy attack or pirate raid. In fact, there is no plan behind the layout of the town. Not that this is any bad thing, since in this way a settlement has evolved, at no point in which is the view of the sea - or its smell - blocked.

Hora is packed full of churches. In the **Orthodox Cathedral** there are some fine icons dating from the years of Turkish rule and a Gospel Book which, according to tradition, was a gift from Catherine the Great of Russia.

The Cathedral was built on the site of a small church ('Zoodochos Pigi' the Life-giving Source, i.e. the Virgin Mary) and took its present form in 1780-7, when the Metropolitan of Paros and Naxos was Neophytos Lachovaris. The Cathedral is dedicated to Ayios Nikodemos the Athonite and Ayios Nektarios. Large quantities of materials from ancient temples and other edifices were used in the construction. It is said that the solid granite pillars were brought from the ruins of Delos. The Cathedral, the slaughterhouse and the Apollo Hotel bound the area occupied by the agora, the public assembly place of the ancient city. The agora had four colonnades with marble facades, arranged in a rough square, with a mass of monuments in front of them. In front of the Cathedral there is the **Local Museum**. This museum includes a section of a Mycenean city, which was preserved in Metropolitan Square, and the remains of tombs dating to the early historical era. One of the most frequently painted and photographed monuments at Hora is **Ayia Kyriaki**. During the Turkish occupation, the building was a monastery, where the monks taught the rudiments of reading, writing and music to Greek children. In the courtyard of what was once the monastery there is a little old church, dedicated to the Dormition of the Virgin, where, according to tradition, Marco Sanudi attended his first Orthodox service.

1. The Orthodox Metropolitan Church.
2. Ayia Kyriaki. 3, 4, 5. Views from the Kastro.

In the old town all roads lead to the sea, but they also lead us to the gates of the **castle** built by Marco Sanudo in 1207. We enter either by the south gate, the 'Paraporti,' or by the north gate, the 'Trani Porta,' or 'Strong Gate.' The Trani Porta and the Portara are undoubtedly the two most familiar landmarks of Naxos.

As we go through the gates of the Kastro we enter what is really another place and age, where tranquillity reigns; there are the narrow fragmented streets, the attractive courtyards with their flowers and the mansions veritable palaces of the Venetian families, with their coat of arms over the door.

A vertical incision in the marble column of the Trani Porta, which prepares us to enter into this different world. This is the measure of the Venetian yard and it was here that the drapers used to measure the materials which they would bring for the ladies of the nobility.

To the right of the Trani Porta is the Domus Della Rocca Barozzi **Venetian Museum.** It was founded in 1999 and is housed in the mansion of the Della Rocca Barozzi family. The history of the museum begins with the passing of the Fourth Crusade through the island (1207), when Venetians first settled on Naxos. Today's museum then housed the Consulate of Venice and was from time-to-time the home of various noble families, such as the Sforza Castri. Today's inhabitants, who are descendants of the Della Rocca Barozzi family, decided to 'open' their house to the public and to share its history with them. Furniture, decorations, household goods, etc. are displayed in the spaces of the museum, whilst in specially adapted areas cultural events, such as exhibitions, concerts, etc. take place. (The Museum is open daily from 10:00 - 15:00 and 19:00 - 22:00.)

Of the 12 castles of the Kastro only one remains, that of the Crispi, the palace of the last Dukes of Naxos. It is known as the castle of the Glezos family, from the name of its last owners, who gave it to the State for restoration as a Byzantine museum.

Lane in Kastro with the town's north entrance, known as the Trani Porta.

The narrow uphill streets bring us to the highest point of the Kastro, where we find the School of Commerce, now the Archaeological Museum, and next to it the Capella Casazza, the Ursuline School, the ruins of the castle which tradition maintains was that of Marco Sanudo, the Catholic Bishop's Residence and the Catholic Cathedral.

The **Capella Casazza** ('house church') was in all probability built in the 14th century, although tradition maintains that it was the chapel of Marco Sanudo. Certainly the founding of the School of Commerce was made possible by the property of the Capella, which showed a marked increase in the 17th century, as a result of gifts from the faithful.

The normal functioning of the Convent and **School of the Ursulines** dates from 1739. However, attempts to set up a school for girls began much earlier. In a document of 1713, Francis Tarillon, General of the Jesuits, mentions that the building of the Ursulines should be simple and convenient. Grandeur was to be avoided because of the great cost and because this would expose them to the covetousness of the Turks. The then empty space in front of the Bishop's Residence is mentioned as the most suitable site. In this position the Convent was protected from pirate raids, and the view was «fine and healthy.»

Since that time there have been many extensions made to the Ursuline School buildings; these led to the creation of an intricate and imposing complex which, until a few years ago, served as a highly successful educational foundation with a tradition of its own. In 1986 the greater part of the School was acquired by the State for cultural purposes. The view from the windows and terraces of the Ursuline School continues to be one of the charms of Naxos. From there and from the various apertures in the Kastro, one realises why it was that at almost all periods this hill was the acropolis of the island.

The entrance to the Ursuline School.

The **Catholic Cathedral** dates from the Middle Ages, but took its final shape in the 16th century.

The floor of the church is of marble, paved with tombstones of the 17th and 18th centuries, with the heraldic bearings of the chief Catholic families of the island.

The wealth of baroque in the sanctuary (17th century) 'frames' a Byzantine icon of the Virgin Mary, which is, perhaps, older than the church itself. The mixture of Byzantine and Western styles in other icons demonstrates that they are obvious products of that Venetian-Cretan culture to which El Greco belonged.

It is worth noting that behind the Catholic Cathedral and next to the Episcopal Residence is the small Orthodox Church of Panayia Theoskepasti, with double-sided portable icons by Angelos of Crete.

1, 2. *Views from interior and exterior of the Catholic Metropolitan church.*
3. *The Monastery of St John Chyrsostomos.*
4. *The Theologaki.*

The Convent of St John Chrysostomos

On the slopes of the mountain that rises above the coast at Grotta is to be found the Convent of St John Chrysostomos and the cave-chapel of **Theologaki**.

This convent constitutes effectively a 'lookout' towards Hora, the sea and Livadia.

It is fortress-like in appearance and was built at the beginning of the 17th century. It took on its present form during the time of the Metropolitan Anthimos (1749-89). The icon of the saint dates from 1818. The central courtyard of the nunnery, where the Church of St Chrysostomos is to be found, with vines overhead, flowers and a spring, has always been a hospitable spot, ideal for enjoying the refreshingly cold water and the Turkish delight ('loukoumia') which guests are offered here.

The convent is close to Hora (three kilometres) and a visit on foot makes a delightful walk. It is also possible to reach it by the route to Engares.

Archaeological Museum

The Archaeological Museum is currently housed in the building of the once-famous School of Commerce, where the Cretan author Nikos Kazantzakis was a pupil.

The lack of schools under Turkish domination led in 1627 to the setting up of the school which, with the passage of time, developed into the School of Commerce for boys, and to the establishment of the Ursuline School for girls.

The School of Commerce was run at some periods by the Jesuits and at others by the Lazarists and the Salesians. The School was considered at its most distinguished during its last phase in 1891-1927, under the Salesians; it had by then completed 300 years of operation. Unfortunately, its rich library, its fine furnishings and its valuable archives were destroyed under the German-Italian occupation.

It is, then, in this building that the Archaeological Museum is today housed. The island's Historical Archive is also housed in a room of the School.

As we go into the Archaeological Museum, what we are entering first and foremost is a complex, cool, sometimes even chilly, impregnable mediaeval building. The corridors, the staircases, the small rooms and the vast halls, the ladders, the windows, each framing a different vignette, and the terrace with its ramparts, form a monument which it is certainly worth getting to know. In addition, the museum now houses the finds from the archaeological excavations carried out from the beginning of the 20th century until today, both from the Hora and from other parts of the island.

These finds testify to the presence of civilisation on Naxos from the 3rd millennium BC (Early Cycladic period) to the period of late antiquity, that is, Roman times. Examples of Naxiot art can be seen here, but we must bear in mind that its finest creations are now elsewhere. The museum has some fine geometrical and classical vessels, blown glassware of the Hellenistic and Roman periods, small objects and 'compacts' of ivory and, on the terrace, the 4th-century mosaic pavement of a house from Aplomata. In the centre of the mosaic a Nereid riding a bull emerging from the sea, whilst there are deer and peacocks in the corners. The Naxos Museum is chiefly famous, however, for two particularly important collections: the Cycladic and the Mycenean.

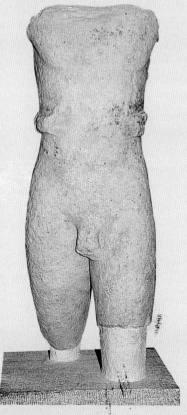

1. *Statue of a female figure holding a wine-pourer. Second half of the 2nd century BC..*
2. *«Kantila,» the only decoration of which was the natural beauty of the marble.*
3. *Body of a marble sculpture, most likely of a runner. Second half of the 6th century BC.*

1   2   3

The Cycladic Collection

Here the sense of the marble makes a deep impression. There are marble vessels, marble idols and even frying pan-shaped marble utensils. It was nature herself, Naxos being so rich in marble, which provided the stimulus for the men of the 3rd millennium BC, and for their successors. This first impression, however, should not lead us to underestimate the earthenware vessels, the jewellery, the obsidian blades and the various other useful objects.

All these finds were funeral gifts, that is to say, they were intended to remain with the departed in their last homes. They were usually placed in front of the face of the dead, or, if more than two in number, they were spread around the tomb, with a preference for the corners. The custom of cremation was not practised in the Cycladic period.

We find ourselves, then, in the Naxos and the Cyclades of the period of Cycladic civilisation, in the 3rd millennium BC and, more specifically, in what is known as the Early Cycladic period (3200-2000 BC). At that time there were settlements on the coast at Grotta and on the eastern coastline of the island, naturally with their cemeteries.

Clay frying-pan utensil with the characteristic engraved spirals.

It is from these latter that we have the finds exhibited in the Naxos Museum, a rich and complete collection. The many graveyards scattered about the island, the careful arrangement of the body in the tomb, accompanied by the objects which had been most treasured in life are testimony to the bond between the living and the dead, worship of the latter, faith in the cycle of life and death and belief in some continuity, some other form, perhaps, of life.

On show in the cases are earthenware vessels from the Early Cycladic I period: cylindrical and spherical pyxides, plain or with incised decoration, and microscopic phials for paints. The clay from which they are made is coarse-grained and often not well baked. The decoration, where it exists, frequently forms a 'fish bone' pattern in repeated horizontal or vertical compositions. The incisions of the decoration have been filled with a white material, giving the impression of a bichromatic interplay of alternating white and dark colours.

Gradually the variety of the clay vessels increases, as does the wealth of the incised and inscribed decoration on their surfaces. Spiral patterns predominate. Here we can see the famous candlesticks, ewers, wine-pourers, multiple vessels, that is, complexes of twin, triple and multiple pyxides and complexes of lamps, utensils in the shape of animals, sauce boats, etc. In their design some of the vessels copy specific models. For example, the pyxis copies the smoothed shell of a sea urchin. On the other hand, the marble vessels are austere and undecorated, relying entirely on the natural beauty of the material.

The pyxis in the form of a sea urchin becomes a type of Cycladic small crater with the addition of a leg and a 'neck.'

A special place is held by the vessels in the shape of a frying pan. It would seem that this type of vessel and its peculiar pattern of handle were Cycladic creations. These are of clay, but in Naxos they are also found in marble. We do not know exactly what their use was, though there are various conjectures: one is that, they were mirrors, the image being reflected in the water, whilst another interpretation is that they were used as drums in funeral processions, a piece of skin being stretched over the opening.

Decoration is confined to the external surfaces; in some cases the pattern of the pubic triangle is incised on the handle. Typical here is a large spiral incised on the whole external surface of the bottom. A predominant place is held by the typical Cycladic many-oared boat with the fish and the flag on the high prow.

However, the most valuable contribution of Cycladic civilisation to art was the idols, which represented the first flowering of the plastic arts in Greece. Marble was used exclusively in these artefacts. In the collection of idols in the Naxos Museum we can trace man's attempt in the 3rd millennium BC to render the human figure.

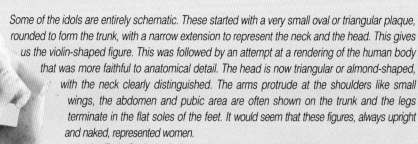

Some of the idols are entirely schematic. These started with a very small oval or triangular plaque, rounded to form the trunk, with a narrow extension to represent the neck and the head. This gives us the violin-shaped figure. This was followed by an attempt at a rendering of the human body that was more faithful to anatomical detail. The head is now triangular or almond-shaped, with the neck clearly distinguished. The arms protrude at the shoulders like small wings, the abdomen and pubic area are often shown on the trunk and the legs terminate in the flat soles of the feet. It would seem that these figures, always upright and naked, represented women.

In the Early Cycladic II phase, the principal period of Cycladic culture, the size of these figures varies from a few centimetres to life-size representations of the human body. The main type of the naked upright female figure has the head in the shape of a lyre, with a triangular nose in relief and a backward inclination of the head, which is supported on a long cylindrical neck. The hands are shown on the breast and the legs are bent slightly at the knee, supported on the tips of the toes.

There are also male forms, more complex and usually seated. The variations and alternations among the individual idols demonstrate the need for exploration and creativity on the part of the Cycladic marble-carvers. These artistic needs eventually led them to the famous 'Harpist' of Naxos, the 'Harpist' and 'Pipe-player' of Keros and the 'Proposer of a toast' in the Goulandris Collection.

There are various interpretations of the Cycladic idols. One interpretation, for example, is that they are figures from Cycladic mythology, similar to the heroes and nymphs of the ancient Greeks. The crooked feet of the idols are thought to indicate that they are dancing and the backward curve of the head shows the figure in a moment of enthusiasm. The female figures, then, are dancing 'nymphs' whilst the male figures are 'heroes' singing in an attempt to invoke the divine powers. More widely supported is the theory that the idols represent a divinity, such as the Great Mother, the goddess of fertility, or that they protected the dead during their journey to the other world. All these interpretations have arguments for and against. What is certain, however, on the basis of the findings, is that in the 3rd millennium BC Naxos played a special role in the creation of the first sculptural arts in Greece, albeit in miniature.

In addition to the Cycladic Collection of the Naxos Museum, the view has been expressed that the 'Goulandris Collection artist' (that is, the Early Cycladic marble sculptor to whom works in the Goulandris Collection, the Naxos Museum and other collections have been attributed) was a Naxiot. He may have been an itinerant artist, there may even have been an export trade in the idols. What is sure, however, is that his works contain the calm, balance and harmony of the simple figures that are now defined by the term 'Cycladic idol.'

1

2

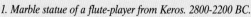

1. *Marble statue of a flute-player from Keros. 2800-2200 BC.*
2. *«The Harp-player» of Naxos, statue of a musician seated on a stool.*

Mycenean Collection

From the large Mycenean city at Grotta and the extensive graveyards at Aplomata and Kamini we have finds of gold, seal rings and, chiefly, vessels with inscribed decoration from the end of the Mycenean period (Late Mycenean III C).

Of the gold finds, it seems that the rosettes were used to decorate
clothing or shrouds, whilst lions were also for decoration, probably of
wooden pyxides. Among the vessels, and. very characteristic of the
period, are the 'false-mouthed' amphorae and the water pitchers
with sculpted snakes and a lateral 'spoon-shaped, perforated
spout'. The snakes are indicative of earth-cult offerings (libations
poured to the dead). Some of the vessels have simple decoration
with undulating or straight bands hooks and spirals. However, a large
group of vessels has decoration based on the motif of the octopus, in
many varied forms, on most of the body and a part of the shoulder. This is
known as the 'polypodic' or 'dense polypodic' style of pottery decoration.

The spaces between the tentacles are decorated with a variety of subjects: free,
abstract design, line decoration and plants and animals. In one case there is even
a human form and mythical beings, perhaps the earliest form of the Greek Pegasus.

Among the abstract designs the rhombus, the pentagon, the rosette, representing the sea anemone, wheels and
spirals predominate. Among the subjects drawn from plants are those suggested by palms, papyrus, ivy, the calyx of
flowers, and particularly of the lotus.

The human form is encountered once only, and then as a small supplementary subject on a 'false-mouthed' amphora
which has as its principal decoration a large octopus. This is the form of a man, with hands raised, in the shape of the
Greek letter 'psi.' The imagery may be depicting a powerful sea demon (Nereus) or a hero traditionally held to have
descended to the depths of the sea (Theseus?). In the Naxos style, since the creatures in the spaces between the
tentacles of the octopus are confined to fishes and sea birds, the decoration suggests
the depths of the sea and some mythical tree of the deep.

Naxiot pottery decoration of the Late Mycenean III C phase, that is, from c.
1200 to 1050 BC, has been described as «the style of the shipowners» of the island,
after the manner of the «palace style of Agamemnon» of Mycenae pottery decoration;
no palace has so far been found on Naxos.

It would seem that the Aegean region, and Naxos in particular, was thriving com-
mercially during this period and was in contact with other centres of maritime trade.
This prosperity is reflected in the finds from the tombs at Aplomata. These seem
to have been directed towards the needs of a community which flourished particularly in the years after 1200 BC, and which continued its
trends towards Mycenean nature-worship. However, new compositions
and new subjects, of Eastern origin in spite of their Mycenean veneer,
make their appearance.

As a theme for pottery decoration, the octopus design evolved in
Crete and subsequently spread through the Aegean, with Rhodes as the
central point. Even so, this design is to be found fully developed and with
an indisputable local character in Naxos (Late Mycenean III C). The Cyclades, especially Naxos, eventually became the centre for its production and
distribution.

1. Mycenean false-lipped vessel with naturalistic painted decoration.
2. Geometric vessel. First half of the 8th century BC.

ROUTE 1

Hora - Engares - Ayia

«We had made the acquaintance of a Mr Lazaros,
a wealthy Naxiot who had a splendid orchard
at Engares, one hour from the main town.
He invited us there, and we stayed two weeks.
What abundance, what fruit-laden trees, what
beautitude! Crete became a fairy tale, a menacing cloud
far in the distance with never an alarm, nor shedding
of blood, nor struggle for liberation. All this melted
away and vanished in the drowsy Naxiot well-being».

Nikos Kazantzakis:
«Report to Greco»

It is true enough that the valley of Engares emits a sense of 'beatitude'. It has delightful orchards, full of pears, apples, damsons and, above all, apricots, the source of the renowned Engares grafts. Here we find four hamlets: Galini, Mytria, Mesi Yeitonia and Langadia.

The Engares valley is the site of the fortified **Monastery of Our Lady Ipsilotera**, also known as **Angelakopoulos Tower**. This was built to serve as a monastery dedicated to the Panayia, Our Lady. It was founded in 1660 by the Greek Orthodox Iakovos Kokkos and was originally directly subject to the Patriarchate of Constantinople.

It is the island's strongest fortification and served as a base and refuge for the farmers of the area in their struggles against the Frankish feudal overlords.

1. The church of Ayia Galini in the village of the same name.
2. The valley of Engares.
3, 4. The Monastery of Ispiloteras, otherwise known as the Angelakopoulos Tower .
5. The Monastery of Panayia Faneromeni.
6. The Bay of Amitis.

We encounter another religious house, dedicated to **Our Lady Faneromeni** beyond Engares. Built in the 17th century, it has fine portable icons and an important library.

We now cross the north-western side of the island; the road runs along the top of steep cliffs, which are indented with inlets with attractive beaches. The most well known, accessible and popular beach is the **bay of Abram**. This is good place to stay for a few days' rest or swimming; one can also eat here.

However, one should not be deflected by the quiet, the coolness and the beauty of Abram from following this route further, because at the end of it, in spite of the heat, a cool and fragrant surprise awaits you.

This is the precinct of the **Ayia Monastery**. Here, amid plane trees and an abundance of fresh water, stands the church of Ayia and the cells of the monastery.

In former times, this used to draw pilgrims from every part of Naxos on the Feast of the Dormition of the Virgin (15 August). The women who had taken a vow to the Virgin used to attend barefoot, even though this involved following rough paths through the mountains.

Before you actually see the monastery, which is below the level of the road, you come upon an unmistakable landmark the mediaeval **Ayia Tower**, standing in a key position and serving as a reminder that this island, apart from its natural beauty, has always been of strategic importance. The road, after Ayia, leads to the most northerly part of Naxos, the Stavros promontory.
The lighthouse can be seen from the road.
We can return to Hora either by the way we have come or by continuing south towards Apollonas and following the Apollonas-Hora road.

1. *The bay of Abram.*
2, 3. *The Monastery and Tower at Ayia.*

ROUTE 2

Melanes - Kouros - Moni
Kinidaros - Potamia

If you want to make a short and enjoyable trip without sacrificing a morning's bathing, then the ideal solution is to visit Melanes and Potamia one evening.

*In the Melanes valley, which is dense with olive and fruit trees, are the villages of **Kourounochori** and **Ayii Apostoli**. The valley took its name (the root meaning of 'Melanes' is 'black') from its black soil. In ancient times its name was probably 'Melas.'*

*The **Frangopoulos tower-house** at Kourounochori is a reminder that Melanes was one of the most important fiefs on the island. Here in a beautiful garden, which now belongs to an ordinary house in the village, but which was once part of the extensive grounds of the tower, there is a marble table with an inscription stating that Frangopoulos entertained King Othon here.*

Our route takes us to Flerio, also known as 'Ellinas', where there is an ancient stone quarry. The name Ellinas ('Greek') comes from the ancient 'kouros' (7th century BC), measuring 6.40 metres, which lies on the ground of the ancient quarry, now in the corner of an orchard.

This colossal, half-finished statue, the Kouros, left lying in the quarry through the centuries, and the kouros at Apollonas are unique relics in the history of ancient Greek sculpture and, of course, of Naxos. Archaeologists speculate that it was for technical reasons or because of changes in circumstances, such as the death of the client, or political events that it was abandoned in this way.

Lygdamis, as soon as he came to power, confiscated all the orders of the rich in the quarries. Soon afterwards, however, not finding it possible to dispose of them, he sold some of them back to their former owners.

These colossal statues are chronologically later than the Homeric epics, which presented the gods in a form very different from that of the old earth deities, who were represented by small idols.

Now the gods were anthropomorphic, but also «much taller than a tall man.» It is precisely this new concept which the kouroi, statues of gods or heroes, express. The popular name for the Kouros was 'Ellinas' the Greek, since it obviously expressed a greatness and power, which could only be identified with the Greek!

It is worth mentioning that the Kouros of Melanes is under the exclusive protection of the Kondylis family, to whom the carefully-tended orchard belongs. The 'Ellinas', the aromatic setting and the local people form a unique composition.

We return to the central road. As we leave Melanes and Kourounochori we encounted Kinidaros, which is famed for its waters - Hora's water supply comes from here - and its songwriters.

1, 2. The Frankopoulos Tower at Kourounochori with a view of the village.
3. Flerio: 'The Ellinas,' the 7th-century BC kouros.

After Kinidaros, we reach Moni.

Moni most probably took its name from the monastery of Panayia Drosiani, which we encounter on the road which brings us from Halki (Tragaia) to Moni.

The **Church of Panayia Drosiani**, formerly the main church of a monastery, is small, with a single nave and three apses. It is crowned by an archaic dome resting on a rectangular base with rounded corners. The church is a rarity for Greece as a whole in that it preserves wall-paintings from before the time of the iconoclastic controversy. The western side of the church was extended in modern times, and to the north there are three peculiar chapels adjacent to it. The most easterly of these has wall-paintings in a number of layers, particularly in the sanctuary. There are a number of successive layers of paintings in the main church, too, especially in the north apse and on the arch over the sanctuary. Apart from the initial layer, the rest can be dated to various periods between the 9th-10th and 15th centuries. According to the experts, Drosiani is one of the oldest and most important churches in the Balkans.

The village of Moni is pretty and, thanks to its elevated location, has a fine view.

From Moni we can reach Kinidaros, which is known for its abundance of water this is where Hora gets its water supply from and for its singers.

Also near Moni is Sifones, a little village which is uninhabited today but has preserved its charm.

The new roads that have been built in recent years provide a choice of route through the upland areas of central Naxos.

The return is made by following the same road towards Hora, but after Ayios Thalelaios, at the cross-roads, we take the road which passes through the orchards of Paratrechos, past the mansion of the Markopoli family, and go up the Potamia valley with its three villages, Kato Potamia, Mesi Potamia and Ano Potamia.

Potamia is famous for its orchards and for fruit of every kind. We then reach Ano Potamia, with its spring in front of the **Church of Ayios Ioannis**.

This is a good place for a rest; refreshments to satisfy all contemporary tastes are available, but one can also try the preserved fruit, bitter orange and apricot, which is produced in Potamia.

1, 2, 4. Views from Potamia with the church of Ayios Ioannis.
3. The church of Panayia Drosiani in the village of Moni,
*   one of the most important and oldest churches in the Balkan*

To return to Hora, we go back by the way we came, although a diversion is possible if we take the Potamia-Trayaia road, following the signposts; this passes below the Byzantine and Venetian Castle of Tragaia. This route provides yet another variation on the image with which Naxos presents us.

ROUTE 3

a) Ayios Georgios - Ayios Prokopios
   Ayia Anna

b) Glinado - Tripodes - Plaka
   Ayios Arsenios - Vigla - Kastraki
   Alyko - Pyrgaki

a. This route gives the visitor the opportunity to travel from Hora along the coast and next to the sea, thus encountering some of the island's most beautiful beaches.

Starting from the beach at **Ayios Georgios**, which was once a neighbouring village to Hora but is now in effect a part of it, we shall embark upon a tour of the countless, entrancing beaches of Naxos, with their golden sands.

The beach of Ayios Georgios.

The road to **Ayios Prokopios** runs through what used to be a salt-pan, in front of the airport that is currently being constructed. This is an unforgettable beach because it is unique in protecting visitors from the force of the wind, however strong it may be. So don't worry if the wind is lashing up the waves at Hora - it's certain to be calm at Ayios Prokopios.

Views from Ayios Prokopios.

Ayia Anna is the next cove after Ayios Prokopios. A short walk is all that separates one beach from the other. To get from Hora to Ayia Anna one takes the Livadia road, or one can go by caique. Ayia Anna is where the potato-seed producing unit is.

Views from the cove of Ayia Anna.

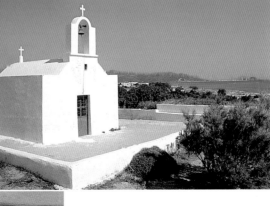

b. We start, once again, from Hora, taking the 'main' road which leads to Apollonas turning before Gala-nado for Glinado, Tripodes and **Ayios Arsenios***.*

Here we pass through the heart of the Livadi - the plain - and the bent figures of men and women harvesting potatoes are to be seen everywhere. Potatoes are today one of the principal sources of income in the agricultural sector on Naxos, although the work of tending and harvesting them is exhausting. Livadi is also the site of the agricultural co-operative factory where Naxos 'graviera' (gruyere) is made. It's well worth sampling!

The name of the village Glinado comes from the family name Glinos, as that of **Galanado** *comes from the name Galanos.*

Tripodes *may owe its name to the votive offerings*

of tripods which were dedicated there. In Athens there is a 'Tripod Street' that was so named because it was lined with similar offerings.

Near Tripodes, on the plain of Plaka, there is an ancient Greek fortress about which there is a folk tale. This tale preserves vivid memories of an ancient Naxiot tradition about the quarrel and eventual mutual murder of Sicelos and Ecetoros, two Lords of Thrace. They had settled in Naxos and had fallen out over the beautiful Pancratis, daughter of Aloeis.

As the story is told today, after the death of her suitors the princess of Naxos settled in this tower at Plaka. She became a prophetess and the tower was her oracle. In the Traditions of Politis we come across this excerpt from the tale, in local dialect:

«After a long time the tower fell down, and since then the maid has been invisible and the light of her lantern has never been seen since.

Quite a long time went past, and then one day, when digging in the ground over here, some shepherd boys found the maiden's three-legged stool in one piece, just as it was when the smith made it and they took it up there to where the village is and everyone came to look, at it, for it was a real sight. And since then the village has been called Tripodes».

The beach at **Plaka** is the continuation of the Ayia Anna and Ayios Prokopios beaches.

Ayios Arsenios (1), Livadi (2), Galanados (3), Tripodes (4), Plaka (background).

This fine beach does not stop at Tripodes either. It goes on to **Orkos, Parthenos, Vigla, Kastraki, Alykos** and **Pyrgaki**; mile upon mile of sandy beach. The particular features of the beach at Alyko and Pyrgaki is that scrub grows in the sand. All the western coast of Naxos has one great advantage: however strong the wind may be elsewhere, here it is always calm enough to make bathing a pleasure.

Vigla can be seen, from its name and its

1. *Alyko.*
2. *The islet of Parthenos.*

3 *position, to have been a lookout post, and large areas of sea and land are visible from here. This will be made obvious if we climb to the top of the hill formed by the rocks. These look-out posts were used in former times to warn of the approach of pirates: fires were lit on them, and the message was passed on by the light of the fire at night and by its smoke in the day. The monuments of the area, such as the **Noskelos tower**, and the place names all bear testimony to history*

3. Pyrgaki
4. The Noskelos Tower.

Mikri Vigla.

ROUTE 4

Angidia - Galanado - Tragaia
Filoti - Apeiranthos - Panormos
Moutsouna - Koronos - Skado
Mesi - Komiaki - Apollonas

This route follows the very backbone of Naxos, as it passes through the greater part of the inhabited area of the island.

As we leave behind Hora and Angidia on the left, the road through the reed beds, agaves and cactuses crosses Livadi, a fertile plan where the potatoes for which Naxos is famed are grown.

After Livadochoria, the central road passes only through Galanado. After the village we encounter the Venetian mansion of the nobleman Bellonias and the Church of St John, or Ayios Ioannis, which on the left is Catholic and on the right Orthodox. This is one of the 'twin' churches of Naxos. From the Bellonias mansion there is a view which takes in all the Livadi plain, the villages of Glinado and Tripodes with its mills, and the landscape as far as Hora and the coast at Ayios Georgios, Ayios Prokopios, Ayia Anna and Plaka.

After Galanado the road introduces us to the real interior of Naxos. We are between Mt Zas and Mt Phanari, with the mountains of Koronos behind. From what used to be the perilous bends of Mitropolo we can see below the villages of Potamia, while the Church of Ayios Mamas stands below the road.

This is one of the oldest churches on Naxos, dating back to the 9th century. It is important for its architectural form, which is 'cross in square', while it has notable sculptures and traces of murals. It is believed to have been the cathedral of the Orthodox before the Frankish conquest and to have been converted into a Catholic church in 1207. Ayios Mamas, protector of shepherds, is regarded as a patron saint particularly of Asia Minor, Cyprus and Naxos.

1. Livadi.
2. The church of Ayios Mamas,
   one of the oldest churches in Naxos.
3. The Belonias Tower in the plain of Livadi.

2

3

2

3

In a little while Sangri makes its appearance to the right of the road, with **Kastro t'Apalirou** in the background on the mountain. We pass close to the 16th-century **Monastery of the Holy Cross** and what is now called the Bazaios mansion. Behind the monastery, approximately in the centre of the slope of Mt Prophitis Ilias, it is possible to make out the Kaloritissa cave, an underground cavern, spacious and impressive, where there are three small churches with unique murals. Experts regard these as being without parallel in Byzantine art. Above rise the ruins of the Monastery of Our Lady Kaloritissa. According to tradition, an icon of the Birth of Christ was found in the cave by a shepherd and this is supposed to be the reason why a chapel was built here.

1. The church of Ayios Mamas, the most important saint of Cyprus, Asia Minor and Naxos.
2. The Monastery of the Holy Cross.
3. The Kastro t'Apalirou.
4. The region of Tragaia.

4

The village of Tsikalario in Upper Kastro.

At roughly the same point on the road, on the left, among the fields, is the Church of Ayios Artemios. The murals, in the form of simple geometrical decoration, take us back to the period of the iconoclastic controversies. of the 9th century.

Ayios Artemios at Sangri, Ayia Kyriaki in the area of the emery mines of Apeiranthos and Ayios Ioannis at Adisaro are the 'anti-icon' churches of Naxos. The decoration at Ayia Kyriaki is enriched with representations of birds with ribbons round their necks.

As we proceed, the landscape gradually changes. There are olives, oleanders and running water, while the air is heavy with scents and the noise of cicadas. We have entered the **Tragaia** basin. This means that we are more or less at the centre of the island, a fact which has always made Tragaia a commercial centre, second only to Hora. The villages of Tragaia, Damalas, Vourvouria, Damarionas, Koutsocherado, Tsikalario, Halki, Akadimi, Kaloxylos, Metochi and Monitsia have a certain unity, but at the same time each has its own individual character. In the western part of the basin is Apano Kastro.

Paths from Koutsocherado and Tsikalario lead to **Kastro**, which dominates almost the whole of the central part of Naxos. From the top one has a view of the whole Tragaia basin, Filoti, Moni and the Sangri area; the view extends as far as the sea. It is therefore no surprise that the monuments show that Kastro was used in antiquity and the Byzantine

and Venetian eras. Thus it has its ancient graveyards, one in the eastern foothills, at Alonia or Alonakia, and another in the western foothills at Sklaves. Tombs with circular stone enclosures dating from the Geometric period have been found at Alonakia. The part which has been investigated, wild and impressive, is particularly striking. There is also a menhir, a single upright monolith, in the area. On Kastro itself there are walls, arrow-slits, 'palaces,' cisterns, fountains and chapels. Until a few years ago, Apano Kastro, an intact mediaeval settlement, was preserved in relatively good condition. Today, regrettably, it is falling into ruins.

There can be no doubt that the dominant feature of Tragaia is its many important Byzantine churches:

Ayios Constantinos at Vourvouria, from the 13th century. Panayia Protothronos at Halki, Panayia Damniotissa at Kaloxylos. The fine murals of **Ayios Georgios Diasoritis** and Panayia Damniotissa and of other churches demonstrate that painting was a flourishing art in Naxos in the 11th and 12th centuries.

The church of **Panayia Protothronos** at Halki is also important for the study of Byzantine architecture, as well as for the different layers of its murals. In the sanctuary of the church are seats for the senior clergy which may date from the 9th or 10th centuries. This arrangement conflicts with the generally accepted view that such seating was a typical feature only of Early Christian times and, consequently, raises new problems for students of Byzantine church architecture. The underlying layer of the murals dates from the 9th-10th centuries and the top layer from the 12th-13th centuries.

There is a wide range of artistic styles. Thus the lower layer of murals consists of non-personal decorative motifs crosses, birds, fishes, etc. In Naxos, as in parts of mainland Greece (such as Episkopi in Evrytania), the tendency to use such motifs did not, however, rule out the use of scenes depicting persons. The 'Frankish' occupation of Greece split the nation up into areas with different influences and so in the 12th-13th centuries mural layers we find local and provincial features rubbing shoulders with innovative new elements.

In 1976 the 15th International Conference of Byzantine Studies provided an opportunity for an exhibition in the National Gallery of murals from Panayia Protothronos, Kaloritsa, Ayios Georgios Lathrinos at Sangri, Panayia Arliotissa at Filoti and, above all, from Panayia Drosiani, between Halki and Moni (see also Route Two).

1. The church of Panayia Prothronos at Halkis.
2. The Ayii Apostoli at Tragaia.
3. Ayios Georgios Diasoritis.
4. Apse of the church of Ayios Georgios with important wall-paintings.

The Tragaia area could be described as 'a little Mystras,' and that indeed was the epithet attached to Sangri by the first Byzantine scholars to study the area some fifty years ago. The description could also be extended to cover the Apeiranthos region.

What is of importance is that the wealth of major Byzantine monuments all over the island demonstrates the flourishing state of Naxos under Byzantium, even though few references to it are to be found in contemporary texts. Occupation by the Franks and Turks and depredations of pirates destroyed or adulterated many of these monuments, which scholars only began to take an interest in relatively recently.

Apart from the research and studies of Byzantine scholars, a major contribution has been made by the conservationists, whose work has involved not only the rehabilitation of the monuments but also the removal of subsequent layers of murals so as to reveal the original one. This work is done in such a way that the later layers can be preserved separately in a museum.

Over and above the monuments, however, the natural surroundings here are attractive too. **Halki** with its neo-classical houses is worth walking round or perhaps the visitor could relax in a coffee shop over a spoonful of preserve or a galaktoboureko. There are two Venetian mansions that of the **Gratsias** family in Halki and that of the **Papadakis** family at Akadimi (see History). One can also go for charming walks at Damarionas, the village from which Ioannis Paparrigopoulos of the 'Philiki Hetaireia', (Friendly Society) descended, and Kaloxylos, which is a veritable garden. As soon as we leave Tragaia we feel ourselves very close to Mt Zas. Its peak, the highest summit in the Cyclades at 1,004 metres, rises in front of us and reminds us of a Naxiot saying:

He thinks he's made a meadow out of Mt Zas!

In other words, he thinks a lot of himself.

1, 2, 4. A stroll through the lanes with the neo-classical houses of Halkis is a true joy.
3. The Gratsias Tower, also at Halkis.

Filoti, on the lower slopes of Mt Zas, has once more become a busy village in recent years. In the past its inhabitants, like so many other Naxiots, followed the trail of emigration, but some have now returned to settle permanently in the village, restoring the old houses, building new ones and investing in Filoti the fruits of their years of labour far from their birthplace.

The Venetian mansion which stands near the centre of the village reminds us that Filoti was the fief of the Baruzzis in the Frankish period. The village church, Panayia Filotissa, is one of the island's finest, with a marble screen and a carved bell-tower dating from 1801.

When Naxos was under Turkish rule, foreign diplomats from Constantinople used to come deer hunting at Aria, near Filoti.

The Platanos ('plane tree') is the bustling centre of the village; an ideal spot for the visitor passing through Filoti to quench his thirst.

After Filoti the road begins to twist up the side of Mt Zas and then leads to Phanari. The air is different here, or you think it is. The road then leads on to Ai-Yannis at Phinelia. The view spread out at your feet here will bring you to a halt; The greater and more attractive part of the island lies before you, with Paros, Syros and the open sea in the background.

Views from Filoti with the Barotsis Tower.

We are now in the **Apeiranthos** region. The village climbs up the slopes of a hill among the eastern foothills of the Phanaria mountain chain, between two valleys with vines and irrigated land.

The village was dubbed 'Apeiranthos' by some unknown literatus a few years before the 1821 Revolution, obviously in an attempt to lend it an air of antiquity. The name as found in popular texts is A-perathou. It is always referred to in this way in the genitive case and in all probability the name is derived from some landowner of the region called Perathos.

The places names all show that throughout the Apeiranthos region, down to the eastern coastlines, there was an abundant human presence in antiquity. Aphikli, for example, may bear traces of the memory of either the Turkish word for some major landowner or the fact that there was a temple dedicated to the hero Iphicles, brother of Heracles, here. There is also an Arsos, that is, Al-son, as the ancients called a woodland sanctuary dedicated to some deity, and a Dimos, a place whose name shows that there was an important settlement here in ancient times. Eiliniko Pezouli was an undoubtedly ancient wall, 23 m. long and 3 m. tall, built with massive unworked masonry, in the area of the emery quarries, The settlement of Apeiranthos is mentioned as an important village as early as 1413 by the traveller Cristoforo Buondelmonti. Its location meant that its inhabitants became emery miners, stockbreeders and vine-cultivators. They still produce a wine which is extremely satisfying both to the palate and the eye, a fact which gave rise to the saying that in Naxos there were springs which produced not water but the sweetest of wine.

The 'marble village,' as Apeiranthos was called because of its marble-paved streets and the considerable use made of marble in the building of its houses, spreads out around two mansions with the Lion of St Mark, the emblem of Venice, at their doors. Until the beginning of the 19th century, these houses belonged to foreign, Frankish, landowners. They are today referred to as the **Zevgolis house** and the Bardanis house.

It is well worth strolling about Apeiranthos. Passing through the arcades and the alleys of this mountain village, you will be surprised by the unexpected 'piazzas' and the cul de sacs, by the great care employed in the details, by the corners of the houses, which have been made into

surfaces suitable for chiselling crosses upon and by the covered balconies, which are reminiscent of sea shells and the ocean itself.

Also eye-catching -on the roofs of the houses- are the 'gardens of strange flowers,' as the chimneys of Apeiranthos have seen described.

The chimneys of Naxos are so varied in type and imaginative in form and construction that it would be difficult to find two alike on all the island.

The particular feature of the chimneys of Apeiranthos is the way in which the local craftsmen build two chimneys close to or touching each other. These double chimneys actually serve the same fireplace and are designed to stop it from smoking.

Among the other sights of Apeiranthos are the churches, with successive layers of murals, dating from the time of the Iconoclastic controversy to the 13th century. The church of Panayia Aperathitissa, with a carved marble screen and post-Byzantine icons, and the little **Archaeological Museum**.

Apeiranthos: the Zevgolis Tower dominates the road towards the 'platsa,' or square. Below: a stroll with a sudden dead-end.

prey having cornered it, or hunters again dancing in celebration of the success of the hunt.

At Aperathou, Manolis Glezos has established the Nikos Glezos Library and the Petros Protopapadakis **Geological Collection**.
The village is also home to the Protopapadakis Library and to a small Folk Museum.

The Aperathou dialect, which resembles the Cretan dialect and preserves ancient Greek and Byzantine features, the songs of Aperathou, particularly the 'kotsakia,' its textiles, its four varieties of cheese and its very ancient customs are often remarked upon. Also remarked upon are the people of Aperathou themselves these mountain islanders, creators of folk art, whether this is song or dance or textiles and embroidery, or even an entire house.

The hard life in the village and the mental agility which is frequently the characteristic of highlanders have driven them to faraway places, where they have not only worked hard, but also studied and made a name for themselves.
For well over a century, Aperathou has been

The exhibits in the museum are from the eastern coast of Naxos and most of them were found by the locals while digging in their fields. The collection consists largely of Cycladic figurines and pottery, which prove that in the 3rd millennium BC there must have been quite a number of small settlements along the eastern coast of the island.

The rarest of the exhibits, however, are the incised slates with representations from Korfi t'Aroniou, also on the east coast, which were found in what had been a small sanctuary and perhaps also a lookout post.

The natural plaques are carved with scenes from daily life. It would seem that hunters, farmers, sailors and merchants dedicated plaques bearing representations of their life and work either to express their thanksgiving for some favour received or to ensure that the divinities were kindly disposed to some of their undertakings. The slates, then, must have had a magico-religious purpose.

The representation of the dance occupies a prominent place. Dancing may have had a ritual significance, but what equally might be represented is hunters rushing forward to seize their famed for the intellectuals, and politicians that it has produced.

Moutsouna is the port of Apeiranthos. Long ago, when the emery trade was at its height, Moutsouna was a busy export harbour. Emery would be brought down from the mountains of Apeiranthos and Koronos, where it was mined, on the backs of mules. Later, the aerial runway was built to do this job. What was the aerial runway? Here are some extracts from the short story *The Aerial Runway*, by Petros Glezos:

They put a railway on columns and steel ropes to clamber over the mountains and bring the emery down to Moutsouna...

To see the iron columns, you need to climb up high, over the mountains which hide them. They are in a line, starting from the Koronida mines, climbing over the ridge, then dipping down to the lower hills and losing themselves in the plain of Moutsouna.

It was hard work. The wagons started from the station platforms, then began to run down the wire, slipping off with it one after the other, skipping over the columns, the mountains, the gorges, and then arriving, still one after the other, at the big warehouse in Moutsouna.

Now the emery travels over the mountains...

And the years pass... and as they do so the emery loses its importance...

Today the runway has worn out and has been very little used since artificial corundum replaced emery on the world's markets. Yet there it stands, a monument to the early years of the Industrial Revolution in Greece.

1. *A pretty plane tree in Apeiranthos.*
2. *The Protopapadakis Geological Collection.*
3. *The Apeiranthos Folk Museum.*
4. *Emery quarry at Moutsouna.*
5. *The coast at Moutsouna.*

Apollo.

In recent years Moutsouna has begun to develop as a tourist resort. Its coves, and the whole of the SE coast as far as Panormos, form one of the prettiest parts of Naxos.

The name of one of these beaches, **Psili Ammos**, 'high sand,' gives the Greek-speaker some advance idea of the dunes of fine golden sand to be found there. A settlement dating from the 3rd millennium BC has been discovered at Panormos, at the spot known as 'Korfari ton Amygdalion.' The plaques we saw in the Apeiranthos Museum are from this section of the coast, more specifically from the spot called 'Korfi t'Aroniou.'

From Apeiranthos the road takes us to **Koronos**; we can stop briefly at Stavros tis Keramotis on the way. The church at Stavros tis Keramotis is the only point from which both the eastern and western coast of Naxos can be seen. On the east coast the **Azala** headland juts out to sea. On the west, at the bottom of the valley, is **Keramoti**, a truly peaceful spot.

A little before Koronos, the roadsigns show a fork for Lyonas, a small inlet, and for the Church of Panayia Argokiliotissa, whose feast day attracts large crowds.

Koronos, on the eastern foothills of the Koronos mountain, is picturesque in its valley of well-watered vineyards. Its inhabitants have long been employed in the difficult work of the emery mines, but as the same time they have always seized any opportunity for celebration.

Skado stands on the mountain slope opposite Koronos. After Skado we come to **Mesi** and, finally, **Komiaki**. All three villages are attractive and a wander through their streets is rewarding. Olives, fruit trees and, above all, vines are cultivated throughout this area, and its wine has a high reputation.

1. The village of Koronos.
2. Keramoti.
3. The cape at Azala.

A short distance from Komiaki is the **inlet of Apollonas** (p. 107).

In the ancient quarry we can see the half-finished Kouros of Apollonas, a 10 metre-tall figure of Dionysus, (see also Route Two.)

Apollonas, the small, old settlement, has undergone tourist development in recent years and it is possible, if one wishes, to find accommodation there.

We return to Hora by the same road or continue along the road from Apollonas to the most northerly point of the island, the Stavros promontory, and then follow the road along the west coast to Hora (see also Route One).

ROUTE 5

Sangri - Ayiasos

There are important monuments from all periods of history in the Sangri area. We have already seen the monasteries of the **Holy Cross** and Kaloritsa, and the iconoclastic church of Ayios Artemios. In the main street there are also houses which once belonged to the Frankish barons. One of the island's oldest monasteries stands in Sangri. This is the monastery of **Ayios Eleutherios**. In 1815 the abbot Kallinicos founded a school here.

The plain, which begins on the Sangri plateau and ends down by the sea to the SW, is dotted with fine Byzantine chapels, most of them dating from the 13th century.

The Monastery of the Holy Cross also known as the Bazaios Tower (1), Sangri (2), the Monastery of Ayios Eleftherios (3).

This is the part of Naxos that we mentioned above and described as the 'little Mystras.'

At the chapel of Ayios Ioannis at Yiroulas, excavations have brought to light an extremely important marble building dating from the 6th century BC, believed to have been a temple devoted to the mysteries of Demeter. It has a square ground-plan and an outer colonnade, whilst another row of columns inside held up the roof of what must have been a spacious, though windowless, chamber in which ceremonies similar to those at Eleusis took place.

The efforts to gather the stones originally belonging to the temple, even when these had subsequently been incorporated into other structures, have been so successful that today it has been possible to rebuild the temple. When reconstruction is complete,

the **Temple of Demeter at Yiroulas** will be one of the most complete and important Ionic monuments, comparable only with the temple of Aphaia on Aegina.

The turn on the main road at the level of the Holy Cross monastery leads us on into the heart of the plain of Sangri. Small Byzantine churches can be seen among the farms; we pass close to the Apaliros castle and reach the sea down at **Ayiasos** bay. Ayiasos was where Marco Sanudo landed on Naxos in 1207; he marched inland and besieged Apaliros, where he encountered stout resistance.

1. The church of Ayios Artemios.
2. The bay at Ayiasos.
3. The Temple of Demeter at Gyroula.

GETTING TO KNOW MT ZAS

Zas Cave - Danakos
Cheimarros tower

Mount Zas was closely linked in antiquity with the worship of Zeus. On the path to the summit of the mountain, there is a block of unworked marble, which bears the ΟΡΟΣ ΔΙΟΣ ΜΗΛΩΣΙΟΥ - 'boundary of the temple of Zeus Melosios,' that is. The meaning of 'Melosios' is not known, but it may be connected with an ancient word for sheep. Perhaps Zeus was worshipped here as a protector of the flocks.

The Zas Cave is to the SE of Filoti on the SW side of the mountain, at a distance of about 600 metres. The cave, in which obsidian tools and fragments of pottery have been found, consists of a main chamber and a smaller chamber.

There is a tradition that under the Turks the islanders used the chamber as a chapel. Perhaps this is the reason why the largest two of the stalagmites that decorate the cave are known as the Priest and the Priest's Wife, though of course there is also a tradition that these stalagmites are the result of divine intervention: God petrified the priest and his wife to save them from being captured by the Turks.

Until some effort is made to develop the area for tourism, a visit to the Zas Cave will remain a treat solely for determined walkers.

Those who like taking things a little more easily will be able to see two different aspects of Mt Zas. The first of these is an outing to Danakos.

After Filoti on the Apeiranthos road we begin to climb towards Phanari. A sign for Danakos leads us up the bends snaking across the side of the mountain.

The little village of Danakos lies in a gorge running deep into the mountainside. Life has always been, and continues to be, difficult here. The village is isolated and the soil infertile and it could be said with some truth that the only source of life is the plentiful supply of water. The centre of the village is the spring, with its plane trees. The

1. Mt Zas.
2. The Monastery of Fotodotis Christos, one of the oldest in Naxos.

villagers, despite the arduous life they lead, are hospitable and friendly.

The **Monastery of Fotodotis Christos** (Christ the Giver of Light) stands above Danakos on a hill with a superb view. This is probably the oldest monastery on Naxos, and its wall-paintings and dated inscriptions are clear proof that it stood here in Byzantine times too. There is a tradition that it was built by the Empress Irene. In former times it was an outpost of the Monastery of Ayios Ioannis the Divine on Patmos.

Our second outing is to the Cheimarros tower and through the mountains to the most southerly part of the island, Kalantos Bay.

Once again we start from Filoti, following a branch of the main road. The road is poor and the area is uninhabited, but this should not discourage the visitor.

As we climb, there is an excellent view over the whole island. The mountain landscape is superb, and the only people one is likely to meet are shepherds with their flocks.

Cheimarros lies about two hours away. The tower is an impressive cylindrical marble structure dating from the Hellenistic period. There is a ground floor and three upper storeys, and the whole building is surrounded by a wall enclosing a square site. The tower is visible from much of the south-eastern part of the island and from the sea, and so it is thought that it must have been a lookout post. Beacons may have been lit at this point to warn of the approach of pirates. Whatever its role, the tower of Cheimarros has been much celebrated in folk poetry and particularly in the couplet form so characteristic of the island.

«0, my heart is like a bower
And Cheimarros' lofty tower!

The tower is what you look like
As towards it now I hike

Oh heart, be like the tower,
Care for no-one, not an hour!»

The road continues to the sheltered bay of Kalantos, where a swim will prove some reward for the difficult journey.

The landscape continues to be mountainous and pastoral right down to the beach.

Kalantos has so far not been developed at all, and visitors should take care to have both water and food with them.

The British historian William Miller once wrote that Naxos had always been the 'pearl of the Aegean,' and that its orange and lemon groves entitled it even more than Zakynthos to the sobriquet of 'the flower of the East'.

However, one must bend in closely over the flowers in order to appreciate their unique beauty.

One must seek enchantment wherever it exists in Naxos, beyond the limits of any guide

The Cheimarros Tower.

The Minor Cyclades

Koufonisia - Keros - Irakleia - Schinousa - Donousa

Although the Minor Cyclades are not especially well-known islands, more-and-more tourists have been visiting them in recent years. The beautiful, untouched beaches, the plentiful fish and the simple and peaceful lifestyle have attracted dozens of visitors. **Irakleia, Schinousa** and the **Koufonisia** are approximately three miles to the south of Naxos. A little further along is the uninhabited island of **Keros**, with its many archaeological finds, and, finally, there is **Donousa**, which lies to the west of Naxos and is somewhat isolated. Amorgos lies very near these islands and there are regular ferry connections with Amorgos as well as with the island of Naxos.

There are ferry connections from Piraeus with all these islands, whilst in the summer there are also high-speed catamarans. There are also 'flying dolphin' high-speed connections from the port of Rafina in Attica to Irakleia, Schinousa and the Koufonisia. From the eastern Minor Cyclades you can visit many of the Cycladic islands and even travel as far as the Dodecanese in the summer.

Despite the fact that these islands do not have a developed tourism sector, the few small hotels and rented rooms that do exist can accommodate a fairly large number of visitors.

There are no vehicles on the eastern Minor Cyclades aside from those used in agriculture.

These islands provide the opportunity, then, both for hiking, since the distances are small, and for excursions around the beautiful, sandy coasts by caique.

Koufonisia

These are two islands, Epano (Upper) and Kato (Lower) Koufonisi. Kato Koufonisi is inhabited only periodically and has a few deserted beaches. Interest, then, is centred upon Epano Koufonisi (where the boat docks), which has around 300 inhabitants, many fishing boats and beautiful sandy beaches.

There are five fine beaches in sequence in Epano Koufonisi. The first is inside the harbour. From here, proceeding in an easterly direction, you will come after 5 minutes to a beautiful, sheltered beach. After another 25 minutes you will reach Pori, a circular bay which one imagines was designed using a pair of compasses, and with the island's most beautiful sandy beach. To the north of the 'arm' of land which protects the bay there is a famous sea cave.

Keros

The uninhabited island of Keros, an important centre of ancient Cycladic civilisation, lies near the Koufonisia.

There are many remains of this civilisation on Keros and the neighbouring islets, and many important finds are now in museums. Amongst these finds are the famous idols (the small marble statues) of the harp-player and the pipe-player, which can now be seen in the Archaeological Museum in Athens.

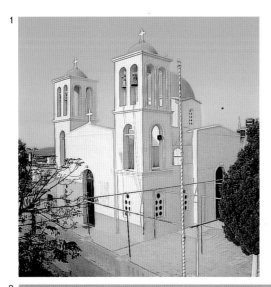

Irakleia

Irakleia is perhaps the most primitive of the
three islands (it has only 120 inhabitants), with
the port of Ayios Georgios, the remains of the
Kastro 15 minutes from the port and the village
of Irakleia, also known as Hora, about an hour's
distance by foot from Ayios Georgios. From Hora
you can visit the Cave of the Cyclops, which is
45 minutes away on the south-west side of the
island. You will, however need a guide from the
village and a torch light. At Irakleia you will find
the beach on the bay of Ayios Georgios, where
the island's port is also situated. The beautiful
beach of Livadi is also 15 minutes from Ayios
Georgios. Both beaches face northwards.

Schinousa

This island has low hills, with the main village of Hora, or Schinousa, in the middle and bays with beautiful sandy beaches all around. One of these, Mersini, is also the island's small port. There is also another small hamlet on Schinousa, Mesaria. The island has 150 inhabitants. There are eight charming, sandy little gulfs all around Hora. The beaches are Mersini (ten minutes from Hora), Tsingoura (15 minutes), Livadi (20 minutes, these three beaches are protected from the northerly summer winds) and, further away, Almyros, Liouliou and Psili Ammos.

Donousa

This island has only 130 inhabitants, who are scattered among the hamlets of Donousa (the port, which the locals call Stavros), Haravyi, Mersini and Kalotaritissa. One fine beach is to be found on the gulf where the boats dock. There are also other fine beaches, such as Kentros, which is perhaps the loveliest beach on the island.

1, 2. *Irakleia.*
3. *Schinousa.*

INDEX

BIBLIOGRAPHY

Della-Rocca, I. *«Χρονικόν της Σχολής Ουρσουλινών Νάξου (1630-1969)»*,
 Epiteris Etairias Kykladikon Meleton D', 1964.
 «Η Καπέλλα Καζάντζα, η Αδελφοσύνη και η Εμπορική Σχολή Νάξου»,
 Epiteris Etairias Kykladikon Meleton H', 1969-70.

Dimitrokallis, G. *«Βυζαντινοί ναοί της Νάξου»*, Νάξος - Tourist Study, 1969.

Efstathou, I. and D. Zevgoli-Glezou *«Υφαντά Νάξου»* EOMEX, May 1982.

Kardara, C. *«Απλώματα Νάξου - Κινητά ευρήματα τάφων Α και Β»*, Athens 1977.

Katsoura, A. *«Τοπωνύνια της Νάξου»* Naxiakon Archion, 6-10, Naxos 1974.
 «Οι Τούρκοι της Νάξου», Epiteris Etairias Kykladikon Meleton I', 1971-73.
 «Ένα χωριό στιχουργεί», Athens, 1974.

Katsoura, A. and N. Keffliniadi *«Νάξος - Τουριστική έρευνα»*, Athens, 1969.

Keffliniadi, N. *«Ο πύργος του Μαρκοπολίτη εις Ακαδήμους Νάξου»*,
 Epiteris Etairias Kykladikon Meleton F', 1967.
 «Η ιστορία της Νάξου μέσα από τα μνημεία της», Naxiaka 1, Athens, 1985.
 «Χριστιανικά μνημεία της Νάξου», Naxiaka 1, Athens, 1985.

Kontoleon, N. *«Εκ της Αρχαϊκής Νάξου»*, Naxiakon Archion 5, Naxos, 1947.
 «Μυκηναϊκή Νάξος», Epiteris Etairias Kykladikon Meleton A', 1961.

Kourourpakis, K., E. Savvari, M. Stathaki-Spiliopoulou, V. Tsamtsouri,
 Ελληνική Παραδοσιακή Αρχιτεκτονική, «Νάξος». Melissa, 1981.

Lambrinoudaki, V. *«Αρχαία Νάξος, Ιστορία και Πολιτισμός»*, Naxiaka 1, Athens 1985.

Mantzourani, K. *«Τύπος και τυπογραφία στη Νάξο»*, Naxiakon Archion 2-3, 1947.

Papathansopoulou, Y. *«Νεολιθικά - Κυκλαδικά»*, National Archaeological Museum, Melissa, 1981.

Petrocheilou, A. *«Σπήλαια της Νάξου»*, Naxos-Tourism Study, 1969.

SLOT B. *«Οι καθολικές εκκλησίες της Νάξου»*, *Naxos-Tourism Study, 1969.*

Vasiliades, D. *«Θεώρηση της αιγαιοπελαγίτικης αρχιτεκτονικής υπό ανήσυχη οπτική γωνία»*,
 Athens, 1972.
 «Βυζαντινές τοιχογραφίες και εικόνες: κατάλογος της έκθεσης»,
 National Gallery, September - December 1976.

Zevgoli-Glezou, Dialechti *«Παροιμίες από την Απείρανθο της Νάξου»*, Laographia, 1963.

Texts (Naxos): K. A. KATSOUROS, S. A. KATSOUROU
Texts (Minor Cyclades): GIANNIS DESYPRIS
Text editor: DAPHNE CHRISTOU
Artistic editor: EVI DAMIRI
Photographs: M. TOUBIS S.A.

Production - Printing: M. Toubis S.A.